Set A Listening Foundation practice paper

Time: 30 minutes and 5 minutes' reading time

Total marks: 50

SECTION A

Questions and answers in **English**

  Hobbies

1   What do these people enjoy doing?
     Listen to the recording and put a cross ⊠ in each one of the **three** correct boxes.

Example	going skiing	✗
A	going cycling	☐
B	watching TV	☐
C	going swimming	⊠
D	reading	⊠
E	playing chess	☐
F	going shopping	☐
G	going wind surfing	⊠

(Total for Question 1 = 3 marks)

Revision Guide
Page 20
Hobbies

Vocab hint

Remember to try to link what you hear to the words you might already know. For example, you might be listening out for **la natation** (swimming) but hear **nager** (to swim).

Listening skills

When you listen, switch on straight away and remember to listen right up to the end of the passage as the answer could come anywhere.

Vocab hint

Be prepared to listen for more unexpected words. For example, there are many different ways to say 'shopping' in French: **faire les magasins**, **faire les courses** or just references to buying things (**acheter**).

Revision Guide
Page 3
Describing family

Listening skills

Listen for French words which mean the same as those in the English multiple-choice options. For example, **cadet** means 'younger' and could relate to a choice about age.

 Family relationships

Listen to the recording

2   Your exchange partner, Malaika, is talking about her family. What does she say?

Listen to the recording and complete these statements by putting a cross ☒ in the correct box for each question.

Example: Malaika thinks that her sister is…

☐	**A**	lazy
☐	**B**	hard-working
☐	**C**	funny
☒	**D**	chatty

(i) Malaika's brother…

☒	**A**	gets on Malaika's nerves
☐	**B**	does nothing to help at home
☐	**C**	is older than Malaika
☐	**D**	is always well behaved

(ii) Malaika gets on well with her mother because…

☐	**A**	she is generous
☐	**B**	she allows Malaika a lot of freedom
☒	**C**	they like the same things
☐	**D**	she is understanding

(iii) Malaika says that her dad…

☐	**A**	is very sporty
☒	**B**	is quite strict
☒	**C**	makes people laugh
☐	**D**	is difficult to get on with

(Total for Question 2 = 3 marks)

Part-time jobs

Listen to the recording

3 Your exchange partner and her friends are talking about jobs. What do they say?

Listen to the recording and put a cross ⊠ next to each one of the **three** correct statements.

		Luc	Paul	Isabelle
Example	I work in a supermarket.	☒	☐	☐
A	I like working outdoors.	☐	☐	☐
B	I work on Saturdays.	☐	☐	☐
C	I do babysitting.	☐	☐	☐
D	I don't like my part-time job.	☒	☐	☐
E	My job is well paid.	☐	☐	☒
F	I work for a member of my family.	☐	☒	☐
G	I get on with my boss.	☒	☐	☐

(Total for Question 3 = 3 marks)

 Future plans

Listen to the recording

4 Your exchange partner is telling you what his friends, Alice, Dominique and Katy, want to do later in life.

Listen to the recording and put a cross ⊠ in each one of the three correct boxes.

		Alice	Dominique	Katy
Example	work in IT	☒	☐	☐
A	travel abroad	☒	☐	☐
B	get married	☐	☐	☐
C	have children	☐	☐	☒
D	become a singer	☐	☐	☐
E	do voluntary work	☐	☒	☐
F	go to university	☐	☐	☐
G	become rich	☐	☐	☐

(Total for Question 4 = 3 marks)

Revision Guide
Page 68
Part-time jobs

Listening skills

Listen for positive and negative adjectives to help you. For example, génial indicates a positive opinion and ennuyeux a negative opinion.

Vocab hint

Je m'entends bien avec… I get on well with…

Revision Guide
Page 63
Future plans

Hint

It is always good to listen out for negatives (ne…pas, ne…rien, ne…jamais, etc.) as they change the meaning completely.

Vocab hint

il / elle veut he / she wants

il / elle a envie de he / she is keen to

il / elle voudrait or il / elle aimerait he / she would like

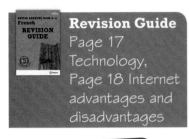

Revision Guide
Page 17
Technology,
Page 18 Internet
advantages and
disadvantages

Listening skills

Make sure you answer in the same language as the question! If the questions are in English, you should answer in English. If the questions are in French, answer in French!

It's a good idea to jot down what you hear next to the question and then check your answers on the second hearing.

Revision Guide
Page 34
Holiday activities

Listening skills

You are really listening for key words here but you will need to pay attention as the passages are quite short. Make sure that you are ready to listen straight away and don't lose your concentration.

Hint

It is always a good idea to read through all of the options given in the box before trying to answer any of the questions.

 The internet   Listen to the recording

5 You are listening to your exchange partner's mother talking about the internet. What does she tell you?

Listen to the recording and answer the following questions **in English**.

(a) What does she do from time to time?

..... Download music ..... **(1 mark)**

(b) Why does she shop online?

..... Easy ..... **(1 mark)**

(c) What did she do yesterday online?

..... Did some research .....

..... **(1 mark)**

(d) With whom is she going to speak next weekend?

..... A friend online who lives in Canada ..... **(1 mark)**

(Total for Question 5 = 4 marks)

  Holidays   Listen to the recording

6 Sandra and Lionel are talking about holidays.

What do they say they do on holiday?

Complete the sentences. Use the correct word or phrase from the box.

plays football	~~plays volleyball~~	goes sailing	sunbathes
visits museums	goes wind surfing	buys presents	visits castles

(a) Sandra ..plays volleyball.. and ..Sunbathes.. **(1 mark)**

(b) Lionel ..goes sailing.. and ..buys presents.. **(2 marks)**

(Total for Question 6 = 3 marks)

Helping others

Listen to the recording

7　During an internet link with your exchange school, Marc tells you what he does to be helpful.

What does he say that he does to help others?

Listen to the recording and put a cross ⊠ in each one of the **three** correct boxes.

Example	babysits for his aunt	☒
A	listens to his friends' problems	☐
B	volunteers at an animal shelter	☐
C	gives money to the homeless	☐
D	does shopping for an old lady	☐
E	gives blood	☐
F	walks the neighbour's dog	☐
G	helps his brother with homework	☒

(Total for Question 7 = 3 marks)

 Helping the environment

Listen to the recording

8　You hear this interview on Belgian radio.

Listen to the interview and answer the following questions **in English**.

(a) What does Simon do every day?

.... **(1 mark)**

(b) What does he say we must do?

.... **(1 mark)**

(c) What is he going to ask his parents to do?

.... **(1 mark)**

(Total for Question 8 = 3 marks)

Set A
Listening
Foundation

Revision Guide
Page 74
Helping others

Listening skills

Listen for groups of words rather than individual ones: un chien is mentioned but is it to do with walking the neighbour's dog?

Vocab hint

faire du baby-sitting to babysit

faire des achats to go shopping

faire du bénévolat to do voluntary work

Revision Guide
Page 80
Being green

Listening skills

Listen for the right words if you can and be flexible. For example, in part (b) there is no word in the passage for 'we' / 'you', so take care.

Hint

Use the context to help you. For example, if you don't know gaspiller, you could guess its meaning from the sentence around it.

Grammar hint

'we must' = il faut, on doit, nous devons.

Revision Guide
Page 47
Describing a town

Hint

Listen for correct tenses in French: question (iii) needs a past time frame and question (iv) a future time frame.

Grammar hint

Remember that perfect tenses always need two parts: je suis allé, j'ai regardé, etc.

 A French town

9   Your French friend, Aline, is telling you about her town.

Listen to what she says and complete the sentences by putting a cross ⊠ in the correct box for each question.

Example: Aline lives in the…

☐	**A**	North
☐	**B**	South
☐	**C**	East
☒	**D**	West

(i) Her house…

☐	**A**	is quite small
☐	**B**	has no garden
☐	**C**	is in the town centre
☐	**D**	has three bedrooms

(ii) In her town you cannot…

☐	**A**	go to the cinema
☐	**B**	go ice skating
☐	**C**	go swimming
☐	**D**	visit a castle

(iii) Yesterday she…

☐	**A**	went out for a meal in town
☐	**B**	went shopping in town
☐	**C**	went to church in town
☐	**D**	went bowling in town

(iv) In the future she would like to live…

☐	**A**	abroad
☐	**B**	in the countryside
☐	**C**	in the mountains
☐	**D**	at the seaside

(Total for Question 9 = 4 marks)

Planning to go out

10 You hear two friends, Annie and Jamel, discussing a visit to a concert.

Listen to the conversation and answer the following questions **in English**.

(a) When is the concert taking place?

.... **(1 mark)**

(b) How much does it cost to watch the concert?

.... **(1 mark)**

(c) What kind of music does Annie not like?

.... **(1 mark)**

(d) What are the friends planning to do after the concert?

.... **(1 mark)**

(Total for Question 10 = 4 marks)

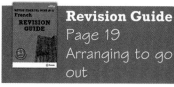 **Revision Guide**
Page 19
Arranging to go out

Listening skills

Don't be put off when two people are speaking. There will usually be a male and female voice so that you can tell when a new person is speaking.

Hint

Focus on the question words in English to make sure that you are supplying the correct type of answer.

 A school exchange

11 You hear your friend, Lucas, talking about a school exchange he has been on.

What does he talk about?

Listen to the recording and put a cross ☒ in each one of the **three** correct boxes.

Example	the journey to England	☒
A	lunches at the English school	☐
B	maths lessons	☐
C	a visit to a theme park	☐
D	the teachers in England	☐
E	a theatrical event	☐
F	a sporting event	☐
G	homework	☐

(Total for Question 11 = 3 marks)

Revision Guide
Page 62
Exchanges

Hint

You only have to pick up on what Lucas is talking about, not a particular viewpoint.

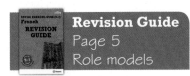

Revision Guide
Page 5
Role models

Hint

When looking for reasons or justifications for opinions, listen for words like parce que, car or puisque to focus your attention.

Vocab hint

je respecte I respect
j'admire I admire
mon modèle est
my role model is
mon héros est
my hero is

  Role models

Listen to the recording

12 You hear this report about role models on French radio.

Listen to the report and answer the following questions **in English**.

(a) Why does Gilbert respect his grandfather?

.... **(1 mark)**

(b) Where was his grandfather brought up?

.... **(1 mark)**

(c) What does Gilbert hope to do in the future?

.... **(1 mark)**

(d) What quality does Gilbert admire in his favourite footballer?

.... **(1 mark)**

(Total for Question 12 = 4 marks)

SECTION B
Questions and answers in **French**

 **La routine**

Listen to the recording

13 Carole parle de sa routine.

Complète les phrases en choisissant un mot ou des mots dans la case. Il y a des mots que tu n'utiliseras pas.

tard   en car   en voiture   théâtre   vélo   avec ses copines
~~paresseuse~~   manger   lire   faire les devoirs   tôt   judo

Exemple: Carole est ……paresseuse……

(a) D'habitude, Carole doit se lever ……………………… (1 mark)

(b) Elle n'a pas le temps de ……………………… le matin. (1 mark)

(c) Elle va à l' école ……………………… (1 mark)

(d) Carole fait du ………………… une fois par semaine. (1 mark)

(e) Le soir, elle n'aime pas ………………………… (1 mark)

(Total for Question 13 = 5 marks)

 Les copains

Listen to the recording

14 Olivier parle de ses copains.

Comment sont ses amis? Choisis entre: **amusant, actif, bavard** et **intelligent**.

Chacun des mots peut être utilisé plusieurs fois.

Exemple: Marcus est ………actif………

(a) Yann est ……………………………… (1 mark)

(b) Hélio est ……………………………… (1 mark)

(c) Olivier trouve Jules très ……………………………… (1 mark)

(d) Son frère, André, est ……………………………… (1 mark)

(e) Victor est ……………………………… (1 mark)

(Total for Question 14 = 5 marks)
TOTAL FOR PAPER = 50 MARKS

Revision Guide
Page 11
Everyday life

Listening skills

Listen for time phrases, which can tell you when things happen. Make a list and learn them.

Vocab hint

d'habitude usually
tous les jours every day
le soir in the evening
de temps en temps sometimes, from time to time

Revision Guide
Page 4
Friends

Vocab hint

Try to find French words which might mean the same as the adjectives in the statements here (synonyms).

Grammar hint

Little words like 'very' are **intensifiers**. Listen here for **très** (very), **vraiment** (really), **si** (so). See page 110 of the Revision Guide for more examples.

Hint

In this type of question you can only choose from the list of adjectives given.

Speaking skills

The role play will last 1–1.5 minutes, the picture-based task will be 2.5–3 minutes and the conversation will last 3.5–4.5 minutes.

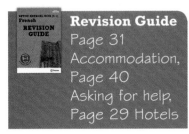

Revision Guide
Page 31 Accommodation, Page 40 Asking for help, Page 29 Hotels

Hint

Remember that when you ask a question, it must relate to the prompt given. In this case, any question to do with parking at the hotel would be fine.

Speaking skills

Once you are in the test, make sure you actually answer the teacher's questions – don't just ignore them and read your notes exactly as you have written them!

Hint

There is no need to use words like s'il vous plaît in the role play as it is marked for communication and use of French – but it might be nice to be polite!

Set A Speaking Foundation practice paper

Time: 19–21 minutes (total), which includes 12 minutes' preparation time

Role play

Topic: Travel and tourist transactions

Instructions to candidates

You are talking to the receptionist at a hotel in France. The teacher will play the role of the receptionist and will speak first.

You must address the receptionist as *vous*.
You will talk to the teacher using the five prompts below.

- where you see – ? – you must ask a question
- where you see – ! – you must respond to something you have not prepared

Task

> *Vous parlez avec le/la réceptionniste d'un hôtel en France.*
>
> 1. Chambre – nombre de personnes
> 2. Étage préféré
> 3. !
> 4. Petit-déjeuner désiré
> 5. ? Parking

Prepare your answer in this space, using the prompts above. Then play the audio file of the teacher's part and speak your answer in the pauses. You can find a full sample answer of another student's response in the answer section.

Picture-based task

SPEAKING TRACK 16

Listen to the recording

Topic: Holidays

Regarde la photo et prépare des réponses sur les points suivants:

- la description de la photo
- ton opinion sur les vacances au bord de la mer
- des vacances récentes
- où tu vas aller en vacances l'année prochaine
- ton opinion sur les moyens de transport pour les vacances

Prepare your answer in this space, using the prompts above. Then play the audio file of the teacher's part and speak your answer in the pauses. You can find a full sample answer of another student's response in the answer section.

Revision Guide
Page 28 Holiday preferences,
Page 34 Holiday activities,
Page 35 Holiday plans,
Page 36 Holiday experiences,
Page 37 Transport

Hint

When answering the questions, try to add an extra detail if you can, such as providing an alternative view or giving a reason for an opinion. You should also describe, narrate and develop your answers in order to gain higher marks.

Speaking skills

Your teacher can prompt you by asking **Autre chose?** (Is there anything else you want to add?) or **Pourquoi (pas)?** (Why (not)?).

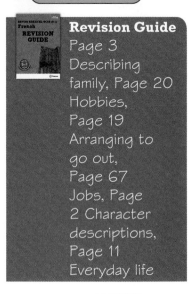

Revision Guide
Page 3
Describing family, Page 20
Hobbies, Page 19
Arranging to go out, Page 67
Jobs, Page 2 Character descriptions, Page 11 Everyday life

Speaking skills

Try to develop all of your answers by adding detail. You can show evidence of greater complexity and range by using different tenses, connectives and intensifiers.

You could also add more complex vocabulary when you develop your basic response. For example in question 1, you could use **cadet** to describe a brother or sister, **m'embête** to show direct object pronouns and **trop** to qualify **strict**. Have a look at the sample response to this task for more ideas.

Hint

Remember that your teacher might interrupt you to ask additional questions. Be prepared for this.

Conversation

Listen to the recording

1 Parle-moi de ta famille.
2 Qu'est-ce que tu as fait le week-end dernier?
3 Quelle est ta fête préférée? Pourquoi?
4 Qu'est-ce que tu voudrais faire comme emploi à l'avenir?
5 Qu'est-ce que tes parents font comme travail?
6 Quelles sont tes qualités personnelles?

Prepare your answer in this space, using the prompts above. Then play the audio file of the teacher's part and speak your answer in the pauses. You can find a full sample answer of another student's response in the answer section.

Set A Reading Foundation practice paper
Time: 45 minutes

Total marks: 50

SECTION A
Questions and answers in **English**

Answer ALL questions. Write your answers in the spaces provided.

Some questions must be answered with a cross in a box ⊠. If you change your mind about an answer, put a line through the box ⊠ and then mark your new answer with a cross ⊠.

 Holiday preferences

1   Read the opinions about holidays on a website.

Janine:	Je vais toujours au bord de la mer car nager, c'est ma passion. J'aime aussi me faire bronzer et faire les magasins!
Thomas:	Je n'aime pas les vacances actives. Pour moi, il est important de se détendre, en lisant ou en ne faisant rien.
Catherine:	Le camping me plaît bien parce que j'adore le plein air s'il fait beau, ou même s'il pleut.
Karine:	Je pense que rester à la maison, c'est ennuyeux, mais les vacances coûtent cher.

Who says what about their holidays? Enter either **Janine**, **Thomas**, **Catherine** or **Karine**.

You can use each person more than once.

Example: ......Janine...... likes shopping.

(a) .... likes camping.   **(1 mark)**

(b) .... thinks that holidays are expensive.   **(1 mark)**

(c) .... is bored at home.   **(1 mark)**

(d) .... likes the beach.   **(1 mark)**

(e) .... likes doing nothing on holiday.   **(1 mark)**

(f) .... doesn't mind what the weather is like on holiday.   **(1 mark)**

(Total for Question 1 = 6 marks)

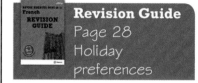

Revision Guide
Page 28
Holiday preferences

Vocab hint

Don't focus too much on individual words in the questions. For example, 'beach' does not appear in the text so look for words which might mean the same, or activities which are associated with the beach.

Grammar hint

Remember that some expressions, such as **il est important de**, are followed by an infinitive.

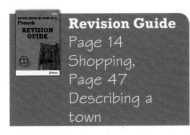

Revision Guide
Page 14
Shopping,
Page 47
Describing a
town

Hint

Make sure that the word(s) you choose to fill the gap make sense when you read through your answers.

 A new shopping centre

2 Read the advert below.

Centre commercial Étoile

Nous sommes à deux kilomètres de Rouen, tout près du stade.

Il y a plus de cent boutiques, un ciné (douze écrans), un grand choix de restaurants et un hôtel 4 étoiles.

Le centre est ouvert tous les jours de 8h à 22h sauf le dimanche quand on ferme à 17h.

Club d'enfants vendredi et samedi, parking gratuit et salle de fitness.

Complete the gap in each sentence using a word or words from the box below. There are more words than gaps.

Saturdays	Sundays	fitness centre	car parks
twice a week	on Fridays and Sundays	~~2 kilometres~~	
12 kilometres	shops	screens	stadium	restaurants

Example: The shopping centre is situated ....2 kilometres.......... from Rouen.

(a) The shopping centre is near a .... **(1 mark)**

(b) There are more than 100 .... **(1 mark)**

(c) The cinema has 12 .... **(1 mark)**

(d) The centre has different opening times on .... **(1 mark)**

(e) There is a children's club .... **(1 mark)**

(Total for Question 2 = 5 marks)

French food and drink

3 **(a)** Read this article about French food and drink.

> Selon un sondage récent, il est évident que les Français sont très traditionnels. Par exemple, plus de 80% prennent trois repas par jour. De plus, la moitié de jeunes dînent devant la télé et une personne sur dix ne mange pas de petit-déjeuner.

Answer the following questions **in English**. You do not need to write in full sentences.

(i) What do more than 80% of French people do?

.... **(1 mark)**

(ii) How many young French people eat in front of the TV?

.... **(1 mark)**

(iii) What do 1 in 10 French people **not** do?

.... **(1 mark)**

(b) The article continues.

> Pourtant, tout le monde pense que les repas pris en famille sont les plus agréables. Presque 75% des Français déclarent manger un casse-croûte entre les repas tous les jours, et les casse-croûtes préférés sont les chips et les biscuits.

(i) What kind of meals are considered to be the most pleasant occasions?

.... **(1 mark)**

(ii) Apart from biscuits, which is the other favourite snack according to the survey?

.... **(1 mark)**

(Total for Question 3 = 5 marks)

Revision Guide
Page 13
Food and drink

Hint

There are several numbers in this passage. Make sure that you identify the correct one to answer each question.

Reading skills

Take care with false friends – words which look like English words but which do not have the same meaning (e.g. chips).

Hint

You do not need to answer in full sentences in order to score full marks.

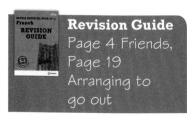

Revision Guide
Page 4 Friends,
Page 19
Arranging to
go out

Reading skills

In longer passages look for clues in the text which can help you to work out the meaning of words that you don't know. For example, do they look like English words?

Hint

Don't be put off by a range of tenses. As long as you can distinguish between them, you should be able to answer all the questions.

 Le Petit Nicolas by René Goscinny

4 Read the extract from the text below.

Nicolas is talking about a recent afternoon activity.

> J'ai invité des copains à venir à la maison cet après-midi pour jouer aux cow-boys. Ils sont arrivés avec toutes leurs affaires. Rufus était habillé en agent de police avec un revolver et un bâton blanc. Eudes portait le vieux chapeau boy-scout de son grand frère et Alceste était en Indien, mais il ressemblait à un gros poulet. Geoffroy, qui aime bien se déguiser et qui a un Papa très riche, était habillé complètement en cow-boy avec une chemise à carreaux, un grand chapeau et des revolvers à capsules. Moi, j'avais un masque noir. On était chouettes.

Put a cross ⊠ in the correct box.

Example: Nicolas and his friends were going to play…

✗	**A**	cowboys
☐	**B**	football
☐	**C**	tennis
☐	**D**	computer games

(i) Rufus came as…

☐	**A**	a cowboy
☐	**B**	an American Indian
☐	**C**	a policeman
☐	**D**	a Boy Scout

(ii) Eudes had borrowed something from…

☐	**A**	his little brother
☐	**B**	his dad
☐	**C**	his big brother
☐	**D**	his best friend

(iii) Alceste looked like…

☐	**A**	a cowboy
☐	**B**	a chicken
☐	**C**	an old Boy Scout
☐	**D**	a policeman

(iv) Geoffroy likes…

☐	**A**	dressing up
☐	**B**	wearing masks
☐	**C**	his older brother
☐	**D**	playing games

(v) Geoffroy and Eudes both…

☐	**A**	have rich fathers
☐	**B**	wore checked shirts
☐	**C**	brought revolvers
☐	**D**	wore hats

(Total for Question 4 = 5 marks)

 An international event

5   Read the advertisement below.

> Au mois de mai, le festival international de la danse a lieu
> à Menton. L'année dernière, le festival était à Brighton en
> Angleterre mais le temps était pluvieux, donc les danseurs ont
> porté plainte auprès des organisateurs. On espère qu'il fera plus
> beau dans le sud de la France. Il y aura plus de quatre-vingts
> groupes cette année.
>
> Pour les spectateurs il y a plein de bons hôtels dans la région,
> mais il y a également deux campings tout près de la ville pour
> ceux qui cherchent un logement moins cher.

Answer the following questions **in English**. You do not need to
write in full sentences.

(a) What was the problem in Brighton?

.... **(1 mark)**

(b) How many dance groups will take part this year?

.... **(1 mark)**

(c) Why might spectators prefer camping?

.... **(1 mark)**

(Total for Question 5 = 3 marks)

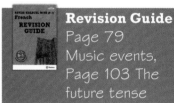

Revision Guide
Page 79
Music events,
Page 103 The
future tense

Vocab hint

Use common sense to
try to guess words
that you do not know.
For example, pluvieux
is used in conjunction
with Angleterre and
le temps.

Grammar hint

The future tense =
infinitive + future tense
endings (-re verbs
drop the final -e).

The future endings
are the same as the
present tense of avoir
except for the nous
and vous forms which
drop av-:
je mangerai
tu mangeras
il / elle / on mangera
nous mangerons
vous mangerez
ils / elles mangeront

Revision Guide
Page 73
Volunteering

Grammar hint

Il y a has two different meanings:

there is / are...

ago (with a period of time, e.g. il y a trois jours = three days ago)

Hint

Remember to give exact answers. For example, question (c) needs a detailed response here.

Hint

Remember that the questions follow the order of the text. You can therefore work out where in the text to find a specific answer, particularly if you know the answers to the two questions on either side of the one you are looking to answer.

 Volunteering

6   Read this blog by Philippe about helping others.

> Il y a un an, j'ai commencé à faire du travail bénévole pour une association caritative qui aide les pauvres en France. Tous les vendredis, je travaille dans un bureau où je classe des documents et réponds au téléphone. Je suis lycéen et je n'ai pas cours le vendredi, alors c'est idéal pour moi, mais à l'avenir je voudrais bien trouver un emploi comme médecin, ce qui me permettrait de faire des recherches afin de réduire les maladies graves dans les pays les plus pauvres. J'aimerais aussi visiter les pays où la vie est dure car je pourrais mieux comprendre les problèmes des habitants.

Answer the following questions **in English**. You do not need to write in full sentences.

(a) When did Philippe first start volunteering?

.... **(1 mark)**

(b) Apart from answering the phone, what does he do in the office?

.... **(1 mark)**

(c) Why does he want to become a doctor?

....
.... **(1 mark)**

(d) What reason does he give for visiting certain foreign countries?

....
.... **(1 mark)**

(Total for Question 6 = 4 marks)

SECTION B
Questions and answers in **French**

 Aller au ciné

 Revision Guide
Page 24
Films

7   Lis ces descriptions sur un site Internet.

Rennes:	On passe *Inferno*, film américain en version originale, sans sous-titres. Réductions pour étudiants.
Dinard:	Au ciné Studio 2, film français, *Alibi*, séances à 17h et à 20h. Ce film va faire rire tout le monde.
Nantes:	Dessins animés pour les petits et les plus grands! Venez voir plus de vingt films à un prix très raisonnable.
Lorient:	Écran 4: nouveau film d'épouvante de Rémy Gallois. Pas pour ceux qui ont facilement peur. Écran 5: film d'espionnage canadien, *Le rendez-vous*. À ne pas manquer!

Quelle est la ville correcte? Choisis entre: **Rennes**, **Dinard**, **Nantes** et **Lorient**.

Chacun des mots peut être utilisé plusieurs fois.

Exemple: On peut regarder un film canadien à ......Lorient......

(a) Il y a un film en anglais à .... **(1 mark)**

(b) On peut regarder un film comique à .... **(1 mark)**

(c) On passe deux films à .... **(1 mark)**

(d) Il y a un film d'horreur à .... **(1 mark)**

(e) On peut voir beaucoup de films à .... **(1 mark)**

(Total for Question 7 = 5 marks)

Hint

Look first at the text for each town and see if there are any obvious answers to fill in. Then look again to check.

Hint

Focus on working out which information you need to answer the questions – there is a lot of extra material here.

Vocab hint

Individual words and phrases can be important. For example, **sous-titres** is vital here. Can you work out its meaning?

Reading skills

At this level, you will not necessarily find the words from the statements in the reading text. Instead, you may have to look for related words which point you towards the answer. For example, the word **comique** does not appear, but can you find other words or phrases which mean something similar?

Revision Guide
Page 32 Holiday destinations

Reading skills

Don't assume that just because the words in the possible answers are also in the text that that answer must be correct. For example, for question (i), **travailler dur** can be found in the text but does it relate to the question asked?

Grammar hint

Remember that to say 'after doing something' in French we use **après avoir** + the past participle. So here, **après avoir travaillé dur** would be 'after working hard' or 'after having worked hard'.

 Les vacances

8   Lis le blog de Chrystelle.

> Selon moi, il faut aller en vacances chaque année car on peut se détendre et se reposer un peu après avoir travaillé dur pendant l'année scolaire. Puisque j'adore la chaleur, j'aime aller en Espagne ou en Grèce, mais mes parents préfèrent des vacances culturelles en Angleterre ou des vacances à la neige en Italie. L'idée de partir en vacances entre amis m'intéresse parce qu'on aurait plus de liberté. Je m'entends bien avec toute ma famille, mais on ne partage pas les mêmes centres d'intérêt. Je crois que, cet été, j'irai au pays de Galles avec ma meilleure copine et sa famille. Nous allons y faire du camping à la montagne parce que nous aimons tous le plein air.
>
> **Chrystelle, 16 ans**

Mets une croix ⊠ dans la case correcte.

Exemple: Selon Chrystelle, il faut aller en vacances…

☒	**A**	tous les ans
☐	**B**	en octobre
☐	**C**	deux fois par mois
☐	**D**	en groupe scolaire

(i) Selon Chrystelle, en vacances on a la possibilité de…

☐	**A**	travailler dur
☐	**B**	se relaxer
☐	**C**	visiter une école
☐	**D**	faire des achats

(ii) Elle aime aller en Espagne car…

☐	**A**	il y a beaucoup de choses à faire
☐	**B**	on peut y faire des activités culturelles
☐	**C**	il y fait chaud
☐	**D**	on peut y faire du ski

(iii) Elle pense qu'on est plus libre…

☐	**A**	avec des copains
☐	**B**	avec ses parents
☐	**C**	en famille
☐	**D**	avec sa sœur

(iv) Elle n'a pas les mêmes goûts que…

☐	**A**	ses amis
☐	**B**	sa famille
☐	**C**	sa meilleure copine
☐	**D**	la famille de sa meilleure copine

(v) Cet été, elle va…

☐	**A**	en Grèce
☐	**B**	à la campagne
☐	**C**	chez sa meilleure copine
☐	**D**	faire du camping

(Total for Question 8 = 5 marks)

Revision Guide
Page 26
Celebrations

Hint

Try to work out the meaning of the sentences before you fill in the gaps. Use your grammatical knowledge to eliminate possible answers. For example, **le régime** and **le service** can't follow **de** in sentence (a).

Hint

Remember that in the Reading paper, instructions in Section B will all be in French, so read them carefully and use any examples given to check what the task is asking you to do.

 Une soirée agréable

9   Lis cet e-mail de Robin.

> Hier soir, j'ai eu un repas délicieux dans un petit restaurant qui se trouve tout près de chez moi. J'y suis allé avec toute ma famille afin de fêter l'anniversaire de ma sœur aînée. Malheureusement, le service était vraiment lent mais la vue sur la rivière était impressionnante. Tout le monde a choisi du poisson, la spécialité du restaurant, et j'ai surtout aimé les légumes. Mon père n'a pas pris de dessert car il est au régime! Dimanche, je vais célébrer l'anniversaire de mon meilleur copain au centre sportif car il adore nager et ses parents vont louer la piscine!

Complète chaque phrase en utilisant un mot de la case.
Attention! Il y a des mots que tu n'utiliseras pas.

mangé	la natation	du poisson	un dessert
~~sorti~~	le service	la vue	la maison
petite	âgée	le régime	l'anniversaire

Exemple: Robin est ....sorti........... hier.

(a) Le restaurant est près de .... de Robin.   **(1 mark)**

(b) La sœur de Robin est plus .... que lui.   **(1 mark)**

(c) Au restaurant, Robin a trouvé ....
     inacceptable.   **(1 mark)**

(d) Toute la famille a mangé ....   **(1 mark)**

(e) Le meilleur ami de Robin adore ....   **(1 mark)**

(Total for Question 9 = 5 marks)

SECTION C

 Translation

10 Translate this passage **into English**.

> J'habite près de mon collège. Ma matière préférée, c'est le dessin car je suis créatif. Je n'aime pas les maths parce que je ne m'entends pas avec mon prof. Hier j'ai joué au foot pour mon équipe scolaire. Après j'ai fait mes devoirs d'informatique, mais je les ai trouvés durs.

....

....

....

....

....

....

....

....

(Total for Question 10 = 7 marks)
TOTAL FOR PAPER = 50 MARKS

 Revision Guide
Page 52
School life

Hint

Take care with tenses. Look at j'ai **joué** and j'ai **fait** and remember that they both go with **hier**.

Translation skills

Think about how to translate adjectives like **préférée**. Where will they come in the English translation?

Hint

Watch out for negatives such as **ne...pas**.

Hint

Watch out for pronouns like **le**, **la** and **les**, which come before the verb.

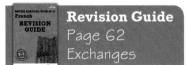

Revision Guide
Page 62
Exchanges

Writing skills

Make sure that you:

- keep to the word count — you may make mistakes if you rush and write too much

- answer both parts of the question — a description and an opinion on exchanges

- keep your answers simple — each sentence must contain a verb, but voici and voilà count as verbs here.

Grammar hint

The present tense of common verbs will be used a lot so revise the basics: il y a (there is / there are), je vois (I (can) see).

Set A Writing Foundation practice paper
Time: 1 hour 10 minutes

Total marks: 60

Les échanges scolaires

1   Tu participes à un échange scolaire en France. Tu postes cette photo sur des médias sociaux pour tes amis.

Écris une description de la photo **et** exprime ton opinion sur les échanges scolaires.

Écris 20–30 mots environ **en français**.

....

....

....

....

....

....

....

....

....

....

(Total for Question 1 = 12 marks)

Un festival de sport

2   Vous allez participer à un festival de sport en France. Vous écrivez au directeur du festival où vous allez.

Écrivez un e-mail avec les informations suivantes:

- quand vous voulez arriver au festival
- où vous allez loger
- les sports que vous aimez
- pourquoi vous voulez aller en France.

Il faut écrire en phrases complètes.

Écrivez 40–50 mots environ **en français**.

Madame/Monsieur,

....

....

....

....

....

....

....

....

....

....

....

....

....

Cordialement

....

(Total for Question 2 = 16 marks)

Revision Guide
Page 78
Sporting events

Hint

Focus on being correct and simple rather than too creative at this stage of the exam.

Grammar hint

When you use part of **vouloir** (to wish / want) it will often be followed by an infinitive:

je veux <u>arriver</u> (I want to arrive)

Learn the present tense of **vouloir** as it could come in useful:

je veux

tu veux

il / elle / on veut

nous voulons

vous voulez

ils / elles veulent

Hint

Make sure that you cover all four bullet points. There is no need to set the answer out as an email – this will be done for you on the answer sheet.

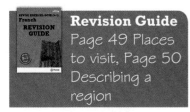

Revision Guide
Page 49 Places to visit, Page 50 Describing a region

Writing skills

- Make sure that you add a reason if you are asked to do so.
- What you write does not have to be true, but try to make it believable.
- Try to keep to the word limit as if you write too much you may end up making mistakes.
- Try to express your own thoughts and ideas using a variety of vocabulary and structures, longer sentences and with correct usage of tenses as required by the bullet points.

Vocab hint

j'habite I live

j'ai fait I did

je suis allé(e) I went

avec mes copains with my friends

je voudrais I'd like

Choose either Question 3(a) or Question 3(b)

Ma région

3 (a) Dominique, ton ami(e) français(e), t'a envoyé un e-mail avec des questions sur ta région.

Écris une réponse à Dominique. Tu **dois** faire référence aux points suivants:

- ton opinion sur ta région et pourquoi
- ce que tu as fait récemment dans ta région
- ce qu'il y a pour les touristes dans ta région
- où tu voudrais habiter à l'avenir.

Écris 80–90 mots environ **en français**.

....

....

....

....

....

....

....

....

....

....

....

....

....

....

....

....

....

....

....

....

....

....

(Total for Question 3(a) = 20 marks)

Internet

(b) Un site français pour les jeunes cherche ton opinion sur Internet.

Écris un article pour ce site Internet.

Tu **dois** faire référence aux points suivants:

- quand tu utilises Internet
- comment tu as utilisé Internet récemment
- les inconvénients d'Internet
- tes projets sur Internet pour l'avenir.

Écris 80–90 mots environ **en français**.

....

....

....

....

....

....

....

....

....

....

....

....

....

....

....

....

....

....

....

....

....

....

(Total for Question 3(b) = 20 marks)

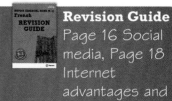

Revision Guide
Page 16 Social media, Page 18 Internet advantages and disadvantages

Writing skills

- Try to write complex sentences if you can do so correctly, using connectives, adverbs and time phrases.

- Keep to the word limit to expand your ideas and write a good answer without writing too much. Look at the sample answers at the end of this book to see examples of good answers.

- Look at the tenses used in the bullet points and reflect them in your writing. For example, the first bullet point is in the present tense, the second in the perfect tense, and the fourth suggests a future tense. You can also use other tenses such as the conditional.

Vocab hint

tous les jours every day

j'utilise I use

j'envoie I send

on peut you can

je vais créer I'm going to create

je télécharge I download

27

Revision Guide
Page 20
Hobbies

Translation skills

Don't assume that each word in English has a direct equivalent in French. In sentence (b), 'goes' does not translate as **va** but as **fait**.

Hint

In sentence (a) there will need to be a word before the French for 'football'.

In sentence (c), remember that saying 'my parents' is like saying 'they'.

In sentence (d) 'listening' and 'reading' will be translated by 'to listen' and 'to read' in French.

Think about the tenses you will have to use in sentence (e).

Les passe-temps

4   Traduis les phrases suivantes **en français**.

(a) I like football.

.... **(2 marks)**

(b) My brother goes cycling.

.... **(2 marks)**

(c) My parents often watch TV.

.... **(2 marks)**

(d) I like reading but I don't like listening to music.

....

.... **(3 marks)**

(e) Last weekend I went to the cinema and the film was funny.

....

.... **(3 marks)**

(Total for Question 4 = 12 marks)

TOTAL FOR PAPER = 60 MARKS

Set A Listening Higher practice paper

Time: 40 minutes and 5 minutes' reading time

Total marks: 50

SECTION A

Questions and answers in **French**

  L'environnement

1 Aline parle de l'environnement.

Complète les phrases en choisissant un mot ou des mots dans la case. Il y a des mots que tu n'utiliseras pas.

beaucoup	énerve	du papier	électricité
le verre	eau	du carton	trop
bruit	les véhicules	~~protéger~~	recycler

Exemple: Aline veut …… protéger …… notre planète.

(a) L'environnement est un problème qui …………………… Aline. **(1 mark)**

(b) Elle pense qu'il y a trop de …………………… en ville. **(1 mark)**

(c) Elle voudrait interdire …………………… au centre-ville. **(1 mark)**

(d) Hier elle a recyclé …………………… **(1 mark)**

(e) Ses parents n'économisent pas l'…………………… **(1 mark)**

(Total for Question 1 = 5 marks)

  **Mes copains**

2 Loïc parle de ses copains. Comment sont ses amis?

Choisis entre: **ambitieux, travailleur, patient** et **optimiste**. Chacun des mots peut être utilisé plusieurs fois.

Exemple: Paul est …… optimiste ……

(a) Luc est …………………… **(1 mark)**

(b) Sami est …………………… **(1 mark)**

(c) Jean est très …………………… **(1 mark)**

(d) Alain est …………………… **(1 mark)**

(e) Georges est …………………… **(1 mark)**

(Total for Question 2 = 5 marks)

 Revision Guide
Page 81 Protecting the environment, Page 82 Environmental issues

Hint

Familiarise yourself with the question instructions by looking at as many Edexcel practice papers as you can.

Hint

Look for clues to the answers in the question. For example, in question (b), the word you need must follow **de**, so you could rule out some of the alternatives such as **les véhicules** or **eau**.

 Revision Guide
Page 4 Friends

Hint

In questions like this one you will need to think of different ways to express the meaning of the four adjectives, as you are unlikely to hear these exact words in the recording.

Revision Guide
Page 37
Transport

Hint

All of the answer options will be possible in this type of context. Try to identify the answers from words you recognise in the recording, or work out the answers you're not sure of by a process of elimination.

SECTION B
Questions and answers in **English**

 Announcements at the railway station

Listen to the recording

3   While on holiday in France, you hear these announcements at a French railway station.

Listen to the recording and complete the sentences by putting a cross ☒ in the correct box for each question.

Example: The next train to Bordeaux will leave from platform…

☐	**A**	2
☐	**B**	10
☒	**C**	12
☐	**D**	15

(i) The next train will…

☐	**A**	arrive on time
☐	**B**	be delayed by ten minutes
☐	**C**	not stop at this station
☐	**D**	arrive from Toulouse

(ii) On platform 9 there is…

☐	**A**	a newspaper kiosk
☐	**B**	a place to store luggage
☐	**C**	a fast train
☐	**D**	a ticket office

(iii) There is a reduction…

☐	**A**	for groups
☐	**B**	if you buy tickets online
☐	**C**	for students
☐	**D**	for under fives

(iv) The train at platform 10…

☐	**A**	will leave without delay
☐	**B**	will depart at 18.00
☐	**C**	has broken down
☐	**D**	will be delayed

(Total for Question 3 = 4 marks)

Talking about the past

Listen to the recording

4 Your Canadian friend, Louise, has recorded this message about herself when she was younger.

What does she talk about?

Listen to the recording and put a cross ☒ in each one of the **three** correct boxes.

Example	her hair	☒
A	the sports she used to play	☐
B	her primary school	☐
C	her character	☐
D	her sisters	☐
E	what she used to eat	☐
F	her friends	☐
G	where she lived	☐

(Total for Question 4 = 3 marks)

  Exchange preparations

Listen to the recording

5 You overhear Louis, your French friend, talking about his preparations for a school exchange to England.

Listen to the recording and put a cross ☒ in the correct box for each question.

Example: Louis went on the exchange in order to…

☐	A	make new friends
☐	B	learn about English culture
☒	C	improve his English
☐	D	visit historic monuments

(i) Louis' friends…

☐	A	were worried about Louis' exchange partner's family
☐	B	asked his mother to remain optimistic
☐	C	thought he would have a good time in England
☐	D	wished that they were going on the exchange

Revision Guide
Page 58
Primary school

Hint

On the first listening, try to identify the points mentioned. Then on the second listening, check your answers and write each cross in the correct box, as in the example.

Revision Guide
Page 62
Exchanges

Hint

The correct answer will not always be spelled out for you in the recording, so you need to listen carefully to what is said.

Hint

Listen carefully to the opinions given here. You might hear all of these ideas, but you need to focus on the one(s) expressed by Louis' friends, not by himself or any members of his family.

Hint

You may hear words such as **puisse** in the recording, which are in the subjunctive. Don't worry too much about them – just remember which verb they come from (**puisse** from **pouvoir**).

(ii) Louis was…

	A	dreading the exchange
☐	A	dreading the exchange
☐	B	worried about spending several weeks away
☐	C	determined not to spoil the exchange
☐	D	concerned about missing his friends

(iii) His exchange partner's family were going to…

☐	A	organise visits during the day and in the evening
☐	B	try to speak to him in English to reassure him
☐	C	help him improve his language skills
☐	D	take him out for a meal every evening

(Total for Question 5 = 3 marks)

Revision Guide
Page 25 TV

A new TV game show TRACK 23 Listen to the recording

6   You hear two teenagers, Robert and Céline, discussing the latest game show on TV.

Listen to the discussion and answer the following questions **in English**.

(a) When was the game show on TV?

.... **(1 mark)**

(b) What did Céline especially like?

.... **(1 mark)**

(c) How do we know that the contestant on the game show was unhappy?

.... **(1 mark)**

(d) Why was Robert disappointed?

.... **(1 mark)**

(e) What does Céline say about game show contestants?

.... **(1 mark)**

(Total for Question 6 = 5 marks)

Voluntary work

Listen to the recording

Revision Guide
Page 73
Volunteering

7 You overhear this conversation in a restaurant in France.
Listen to the conversation and answer the questions **in English**.

(a) Why would the boy do voluntary work?

....

.... **(1 mark)**

(b) For what reason would he not do voluntary work?

....

.... **(1 mark)**

(c) What would the girl hope to gain from doing voluntary work?
Give **two** details.

....

.... **(2 marks)**

(d) Give **one** reason why her friend would do voluntary work.

.... **(1 mark)**

(Total for Question 7 = 5 marks)

Hint

In this question, you will have to think very carefully. The passages are demanding and you will be asked to identify reasons for actions, which might be rather tricky.

 **Extreme sports**

Listen to the recording

Revision Guide
Page 22 Sport

8 You hear a radio phone-in show about extreme sports.
Listen to the recording and put a cross ⊠ in the correct box for each question.

Example: Sylvain tried bungee jumping…

☐	**A**	last year
☐	**B**	last week
☒	**C**	2 years ago
☐	**D**	2 days ago

Part (a)

(i) He wanted to try extreme sports to…

☐	**A**	test his limits
☐	**B**	feel fitter
☐	**C**	feel afraid
☐	**D**	overcome his fear of heights

(ii) He found the experience…

☐	**A**	awful
☐	**B**	really frightening
☐	**C**	quite good
☐	**D**	very exciting

(iii) He thinks that lots of his friends would like to do extreme sports because…

☐	**A**	they might see themselves on TV
☐	**B**	they have read about them
☐	**C**	they have been influenced by his experience
☐	**D**	they are keen to try out what they have seen

Part (b)

(i) Marianne would like to try paragliding…

☐	**A**	as her friends have recommended it to her
☐	**B**	even though it is dangerous
☐	**C**	to overcome injury problems she has had
☐	**D**	because her parents say it is sensational

(ii) She thinks that she will soon be ready to…

☐	**A**	try ski jumping
☐	**B**	try sky diving
☐	**C**	attempt a new winter sport
☐	**D**	become a pilot

(iii) She thinks extreme winter sports are…

☐	**A**	fun
☐	**B**	interesting
☐	**C**	too dangerous
☐	**D**	boring

(Total for Question 8 = 6 marks)

Vocab hint

Focus on the context to work out meaning. If you are not sure about **un vol libre**, first see if you can rule out any of the options. Then think about the meaning of **vol** and **libre** and try to work out what it might mean.

Eating habits

9 You hear this interview on Belgian radio.

Listen to the interview and answer the following questions **in English**.

Part (a)

(i) Why does Mme Moulin think that Belgians are traditional?

.... **(1 mark)**

(ii) What is the presenter's reaction to her findings?

.... **(1 mark)**

(iii) What percentage of young Belgians do not want to eat as a family?

.... **(1 mark)**

(iv) What does one third of this group do only once a week?

.... **(1 mark)**

(v) Which group of people finds eating dinner a pleasurable time?

.... **(1 mark)**

Part (b)

(i) What does Mme Moulin often do in the morning?

.... **(1 mark)**

(ii) What reason does she give for doing this?

.... **(1 mark)**

(iii) What will Mme Moulin do in the future? Give **two** details.

....

.... **(2 marks)**

(iv) What is the interviewer's weakness?

.... **(1 mark)**

(Total for Question 9 = 10 marks)

Revision Guide
Page 12
Meals at home

Vocab hint

Remember the quantity words which are relevant to surveys. Here, for example, you might focus on la moitié and un tiers.

Grammar hint

Remember some of the different forms of the negative which you will hear in this question:

ne...rien nothing

ne...pas not

ne...que only

ne...plus no longer

Revision Guide
Page 27
Festivals

Hint

If there are phrases which you do not fully understand in a passage, try picking out individual words to help. For example, *territoires* looks like 'territories' and *mer* is 'sea'.

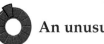 An unusual festival

10 While on the internet, you hear an advertisement for a different kind of competition.

Put a cross ☒ in each one of the **two** correct boxes for each question.

(i) What do we learn about the competition?

Example	It is free to enter.	☒
A	It is the first round of the competition.	☐
B	The competition involves attending lectures.	☐
C	It will take place at the end of April.	☐
D	Children over 7 cannot enter.	☐
E	It is only open to teenagers who live in Rouen.	☐

(2 marks)

(ii) What else are we told about the competition?

A	The aim is to remind children that reading can be fun.	☐
B	The contestants have to write a short story.	☐
C	The contestants have to show their love of reading.	☐
D	The winners have to share their prize with the audience.	☐
E	The winners will get the chance to have a book published.	☐

(2 marks)

(Total for Question 10 = 4 marks)
TOTAL FOR PAPER = 50 MARKS

Set A Speaking Higher practice paper

Time: 22–24 minutes (total), which includes 12 minutes' preparation time

Role play

Topic: At school

Instructions to candidates

You are talking to your French exchange partner about school. The teacher will play the role of your exchange partner and will speak first.

You should address your exchange partner as *tu*.

You will talk to the teacher using the five prompts below.

- where you see – ? – you must ask a question
- where you see – ! – you must respond to something you have not prepared

Task

> ***Tu parles avec ton ami(e) français(e) du collège et du futur.***
>
> 1. Échanges – opinion
> 2. !
> 3. Rapports avec profs
> 4. ? Uniforme scolaire – opinion
> 5. ? Projets en septembre

Prepare your answer in this space, using the prompts above. Then play the audio file of the teacher's part and speak your answer in the pauses. You can find a full sample answer of another student's response in the answer section.

Speaking skills

The role play will last 2–2.5 minutes, the picture-based task will be 3–3.5 minutes and the conversation will last 5–6 minutes.

Revision Guide
Page 62
Exchanges

Hint

Remember that you will have to ask **two** questions at Higher tier, so practise these in advance.

Hint

You may ask your teacher to repeat any part of the role play but he / she cannot rephrase anything.

Revision Guide
Page 81
Protecting the environment

Revision Guide Page 81 Protecting the environment

Hint

You may make notes in the 12 minutes' preparation time on one side of A4 paper. Make sure you use this time wisely; note down some key notes or phrases to do with the topic you have been given that might be useful in your conversation.

Hint

In the picture-based task you might find it useful to think of PALM: **P**eople, **A**ction, **L**ocation and **M**ood. You might also mention the weather and you could also refer to the different colours you see.

Speaking skills

Your teacher can prompt you by asking **Autre chose?** (Is there anything else you want to add?) or **Pourquoi (pas)?** (Why (not)?).

Picture-based task

Listen to the recording

Topic: Environmental issues

Regarde la photo et prépare des réponses sur les points suivants:

- la description de la photo
- ton opinion sur le recyclage
- ce que tu as fait pour protéger l'environnement
- ta région idéale
- !

Prepare your answer in this space, using the prompts above. Then play the audio file of the teacher's part and speak your answer in the pauses. You can find a full sample answer of another student's response in the answer section.

Conversation

Listen to the recording

1 Qu'est-ce que c'est un bon ami?
2 Qu'est-ce que tu as fait récemment avec tes copains?
3 Est-ce que tu vas sortir avec ta famille ce week-end?
4 Qu'est-ce que tu aimes manger et boire? Pourquoi?
5 Comment as-tu fêté Noël l'année dernière?
6 Qu'est-ce que tu aimerais changer dans ta vie?

Prepare your answer in this space, using the prompts above. Then play the audio file of the teacher's part and speak your answer in the pauses. You can find a full sample answer of another student's response in the answer section.

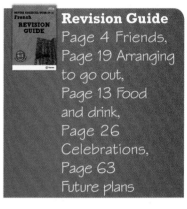

Revision Guide
Page 4 Friends,
Page 19 Arranging to go out,
Page 13 Food and drink,
Page 26 Celebrations,
Page 63 Future plans

Speaking skills

Remember to answer the question which is asked, not the one you hoped would be asked. You can, however, develop answers in an interesting way to help you say what you have prepared. For example, having briefly answered question 1, you could go on to talk about your best friend and what he / she is like.

Set A Reading Higher practice paper
Time: 1 hour

Total marks: 50

Answer ALL questions. Write your answers in the spaces provided.

Some questions must be answered with a cross in a box ☒. If you change your mind about an answer, put a line through the box ☒ and then mark your new answer with a cross ☒.

SECTION A
Questions and answers in **English**

 French schools

Revision Guide
Page 52
School life

Hint

Don't forget to answer in English. French answers will not count!

Vocab hint

Look for vocabulary markers to help you find the right part of the text to answer each question. For example, look for a word meaning 'weird' or 'strange' for question (c).

1   Read what Amandine has written on an online forum.

> Mon collège ne me plaît pas. Les profs nous donnent trop de devoirs. Hier, j'utilisais mon portable en classe pour chercher un mot dans le petit dico électronique et mon prof d'anglais m'a donné une retenue. J'ai dû copier des lignes et il a aussi confisqué mon portable. De plus, on n'a pas le droit de porter de bijoux, ce que je trouve bizarre. J'en ai vraiment marre.

Answer the following questions **in English**. You do not need to write in full sentences.

(a) What does Amandine say about her teachers?

.... **(1 mark)**

(b) Why did she get a detention?

.... **(1 mark)**

(c) What does she find weird?

.... **(1 mark)**

(Total for Question 1 = 3 marks)

Music

 Revision Guide
Page 21 Music

2 Read the extract from the article about the group Daft Punk.

> Dès leur début, les Daft Punk ont fait partie des artistes français les mieux représentés à l'étranger. Les célèbres robots (car ils refusent de montrer leur identité et portent toujours des casques) ont été parmi les premiers Français de leur génération à faire danser dans les clubs mondiaux. Donc, il n'est pas étonnant de noter qu'ils ont eu des problèmes de se sentir français, surtout après avoir signé directement avec le label américain, Columbia.
>
> Grâce au succès de leur dernier album (vendu 3 millions d'exemplaires dans le monde), le duo casqué a réussi à s'implanter aussi bien aux Etats-Unis qu'ailleurs.
>
> À l'avenir le groupe espère faire plus de concerts dans son pays natal et on vient d'annoncer deux nouvelles chansons écrites exclusivement en français.

Answer the following questions **in English**. You do not need to write in full sentences.

(a) Why are the members of the group described as robots?
Give **one** detail.

....

.... **(1 mark)**

(b) Give **one** reason why the group has had difficulty in feeling French.

....

.... **(1 mark)**

(c) What do they hope to do to increase their popularity in France?
Give **two** details.

....

....

.... **(2 marks)**

(Total for Question 2 = 4 marks)

Hint

When looking at texts like this, there will be lots of adjectives. Remember that in French they normally come after the word they describe (e.g. *son pays natal, le duo casqué*) but that they can sometimes come in front as in English (e.g. *les premiers Français*).

Hint

Venir de + the infinitive means to have just done something. It can be used in the present tense to mean 'has / have just' or in the imperfect tense to mean 'had just'.

Revision Guide
Page 53
School day

Vocab hint

There may be some unfamiliar words in literary extracts such as this, but think about the type of words you need to answer each question to help you. For example, if you are looking for the French for 'servant' in the passage, it must follow le or un if it is masculine or la or une if feminine.

 Madame Bovary by Gustave Flaubert

3   Read the extract from the text.
Charles is a young boy who is at a boarding school.

> Charles était un garçon de tempérament modéré, qui jouait aux récréations, travaillait à l'étude, écoutant en classe, dormant bien au dortoir, mangeant bien au réfectoire. Il n'avait qu'un ami, le fils d'un épicier qui avait été envoyé au pensionnat par sa famille.
>
> Le soir de chaque jeudi, Charles écrivait une longue lettre à sa mère, avec de l'encre rouge, puis il repassait ses cahiers ou bien lisait un vieux volume historique qu'on avait laissé à la bibliothèque de l'école. En promenade il bavardait seulement avec le domestique, qui était de la campagne comme lui.
>
> (Adapted and abridged from *Madame Bovary* by Gustave Flaubert).

Answer the following questions **in English**. You do not need to write in full sentences.

(a) Give **two** examples of how Charles was considered to be a normal pupil.

....

....

.... **(2 marks)**

(b) How do we know that he was not popular at school?

.... **(1 mark)**

(c) What did Charles do first, every Thursday evening?

.... **(1 mark)**

(d) What did he have in common with the servant?

.... **(1 mark)**

(Total for Question 3 = 5 marks)

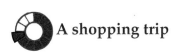 **A shopping trip**

Revision Guide
Page 43
Buying gifts

4 Read Antoine's blog post.

> Ayant décidé de faire les magasins hier, je me suis rendu compte que, puisque j'étais tout seul, c'était une occasion d'acheter des cadeaux pour mon frère qui fêtera demain ses dix-huit ans et pour ma mère qui va célébrer son anniversaire le mois prochain. Mon père m'a emmené au centre-ville en voiture avant de partir au travail, mais j'ai cherché en vain un roman que mon frère voulait depuis longtemps. J'ai enfin réussi à lui acheter un maillot de foot de son équipe préférée à un prix très élevé!
>
> Après avoir pris un déjeuner rapide, j'ai passé une demi-heure dans une bijouterie où je cherchais sans succès une bague en argent pour ma mère. J'étais vraiment déçu, mais en rentrant chez moi à pied, j'ai remarqué une belle écharpe en soie dans la vitrine d'un petit magasin caritatif du coin. J'ai appelé ma sœur pour savoir son opinion car c'était un habit d'occasion, mais elle m'a dit de l'acheter, alors j'étais ravi d'avoir trouvé deux bons cadeaux pour ma famille!

Put a cross ⊠ in the correct box.

Example: Antoine realised that he could buy presents for his family…

☐	**A**	because he had saved enough money
☒	**B**	because he was on his own
☐	**C**	because he was feeling generous
☐	**D**	because he had won some money

(i) His brother…

☐	**A**	has a birthday next month
☐	**B**	will soon be 17
☐	**C**	has just turned 18
☐	**D**	will soon be 18

(ii) His Dad took him into town…

☐	**A**	on his way to work
☐	**B**	before breakfast
☐	**C**	because he was going shopping too
☐	**D**	after he had finished work

Vocab hint

Try to remember useful phrases for your own speaking and writing exams while revising. For example, it could be useful to remember the phrase je me suis rendu compte que and the adjectives déçu and ravi.

Reading skills

This passage is full of alternative answers so you have to work hard to find the correct ones. Read the questions and the text carefully and you will be able to identify both correct and incorrect answers.

Grammar hint

Using ayant + a past participle can translate the English 'having done something'.

(iii) Antoine wanted to buy his brother…

☐	**A**	a football shirt
☐	**B**	a novel
☐	**C**	an Italian shirt
☐	**D**	a football

(iv) He was disappointed because…

☐	**A**	he could not find a ring
☐	**B**	he didn't have enough money for the present he wanted for his mum
☐	**C**	he could not find a scarf
☐	**D**	he did not have enough money

(v) He phoned his sister because…

☐	**A**	she wanted him to buy a silver bag
☐	**B**	he wanted to check that she had not bought the same present
☐	**C**	he was concerned about buying a second-hand scarf
☐	**D**	spending money was his bad habit

(Total for Question 4 = 5 marks)

 **Future jobs**

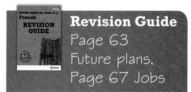

Revision Guide
Page 63
Future plans,
Page 67 Jobs

5 Read what these teenagers say about future jobs.

> Louise, 17 ans, ne sait pas du tout ce qu'elle veut faire plus tard dans la vie.
>
> Annie, 16 ans, a envie de devenir coiffeuse. Elle sait que plein de gens disent que c'est un métier qui ne sert à rien, mais elle voudrait bien rencontrer beaucoup de gens et développer des amitiés qui pourraient durer longtemps, car elle apprécie vraiment la valeur qu'on attache à l'amitié de nos jours.
>
> Les parents de René, 18 ans, veulent qu'il soit chirurgien comme son oncle. Mais lui pense qu'il n'est pas doué. Il préférerait travailler dans l'informatique mais il sait que c'est un secteur populaire, surtout chez les jeunes.
>
> Kevin, 17 ans, aimerait poursuivre une carrière qui conviendrait à ses compétences dont la créativité est la principale. Il croit qu'il sera architecte, mais il comprend qu'il faut travailler dur tout le temps et qu'il risque d'être blessé par des chutes d'objets lourds.
>
> Ellie, 19 ans, a toujours rêvé de devenir chanteuse, mais ses copines se moquent d'elle en disant qu'elle devrait être plus réaliste. Elles disent qu'elle doit penser à un emploi dans un bureau!
>
> Ce qui est certain, c'est qu'il faut choisir un emploi qu'on aime et qu'on devrait faire des recherches avant de décider ce qu'on fera dans la vie.

Who says what about future jobs?

Enter either **Annie**, **René**, **Kevin** or **Ellie** in the gaps below.

(a) .... does not want to follow a family career path.

(1 mark)

(b) .... would like a job which could help forge
friendships. **(1 mark)**

(c) .... wants to choose a career which suits his /
her skills. **(1 mark)**

(d) .... would like to follow his / her dreams. **(1 mark)**

Answer the following question **in English**.

(e) Which **two** pieces of advice are given to people about their future jobs?

....

.... **(2 marks)**

(Total for Question 5 = 6 marks)

Reading skills

When there are separate sections to read, try to finish them all before reading the questions. Then go back and look at them again to pick up on specific answers.

Revision Guide
Page 74
Helping others

Reading skills

Remember to use the language in the questions to help you understand the passage.

Hint

Most, or even all, of the alternatives in part (i) seem plausible so take care to eliminate them by examining the text carefully.

 **Homelessness**

6 Read the article from a magazine.

> Sylvie Martin habite à Lyon, une grande ville où il y a plus de 8000 personnes sans domicile fixe qui vivent dans les rues de la ville. Elle vient de commencer à aider les sans-abri en travaillant pour une association caritative de la région. Le nombre de volontaires augmente lentement mais on pourrait certainement faire plus afin d'améliorer le mode de vie de ces pauvres.
>
> Elle exprime ses sentiments: «J'étais choquée par le nombre de SDF dans la ville. Il y a des jeunes et des gens plus âgés, mais ils ont tous besoin d'aide. Ils n'ont pas les moyens de se nourrir mais il est possible de les aider. On pourrait leur offrir non seulement de l'argent mais aussi leur parler car tout le monde a le droit d'être respecté.»
>
> Tous les samedis elle fait du bénévolat dans les rues où elle distribue des choses indispensables comme des sacs de couchage, des couvertures et des aliments. Mais l'association a besoin d'argent et de plus de volontaires, alors pouvez-vous faire une différence et qu'est-ce que vous allez faire afin d'aider les autres?

(i) What does this article tell us?

Put a cross ⊠ next to each one of the **three** correct boxes.

Example	There are over 8000 homeless people in Lyon.	☒
A	Homelessness can affect the young.	☐
B	Sylvie has always worked for a charity.	☐
C	Sylvie was not surprised by the number of homeless people.	☐
D	She works once a week to help the homeless.	☐
E	She sometimes gives out blankets to the people in the street.	☐
F	She sometimes gives out money to the homeless.	☐
G	The charity has enough volunteers.	☐

(3 marks)

Answer the following question **in English**.

(ii) Which **two** questions is the reader asked at the end of the article?

....

.... **(2 marks)**

(Total for Question 6 = 5 marks)

SECTION B
Questions and answers in **French**

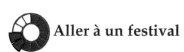 **Aller à un festival**

7   Lis ces descriptions sur un site touristique.

 **Revision Guide**
Page 27
Festivals

Rennes:	Le festival de la culture bretonne se passera comme toujours en avril cette année. On va célébrer la gastronomie de la région. Venez goûter tous les plats typiques!
Montpellier:	Vous aimez les sports de neige? Alors le festival de la mer n'est pas pour vous! Par contre, si vous voulez essayer un nouveau sport nautique, pourquoi ne pas venir à ce festival qui aura lieu pour la première fois en juillet?
Caen:	Pour ceux qui se passionnent pour le passé: visitez le festival de la vie au Moyen Âge en octobre. L'année dernière, on a découvert tous les secrets de la vie d'un moine à cette époque, mais cette année on verra comment vivaient les rois!
Lille:	Le festival de l'art africain aura lieu en septembre. Le dernier festival a réussi à attirer plus de cinq mille visiteurs et on espère dépasser ce chiffre cette année.

Reading skills

You won't necessarily see the words from the sentences in the reading text. Instead, you will need to look out for synonyms and other phrases which will help you link each sentence to the correct town. For example, the text doesn't refer directly to un *nouveau festival*, but it does mention a festival which will take place 'for the first time'.

Quelle est la ville correcte? Choisis entre: **Rennes**, **Montpellier**, **Caen** et **Lille**.

Chacun des mots peut être utilisé plusieurs fois.

Exemple: Si vous appréciez l'art, allez à ....Lille..........

(a) Un nouveau festival se passera à ....   **(1 mark)**

(b) Si vous aimez bien manger, allez à ....   **(1 mark)**

(c) Si vous aimez l'histoire, visitez ....   **(1 mark)**

(d) Le festival de l'année dernière à .... était
     populaire.   **(1 mark)**

(e) Si vous voulez être plus actif, allez à .... **(1 mark)**

(Total for Question 7 = 5 marks)

Revision Guide
Page 33 Travel

Vocab hint

If you can't remember or don't know the meaning of a word such as bouscule in an exam, first check whether you need it to answer a question. If you do, look at the surrounding words – what might happen in the metro at rush hour? When revising, try to look up words you don't know, as you might encounter them another time, or could use them in your own French.

La vie à Montréal

8   Lis le blog de Paul.

Ce qui me plaît vraiment, c'est voyager partout dans le monde afin d'élargir mes horizons. Je viens de passer mes vacances en France. De retour dans ma ville natale, Montréal, j'ai recommencé à apprécier ses charmes. Quand on croise le regard d'un passant, il sourit immédiatement et on te tutoie sans hésitation. Les touristes sont toujours les bienvenus. Dès qu'on remarque un touriste avec une carte ouverte, quelqu'un vient lui demander s'il a besoin d'aide.

À Montréal, on ne court pas et on ne se bouscule jamais dans le métro, même aux heures de pointe. On célèbre la première neige avec la même ferveur que les premières températures positives – le moment où il fait plus de dix degrés, c'est l'été!

Montréal n'est pas une ville parfaite. Je déteste les embouteillages interminables et je voudrais qu'on développe suffisamment les transports en commun, mais la ville, à l'image de ses habitants, est chaleureuse, reconnaissante de son histoire mais tournée vers l'avenir, ouverte, cosmopolite et délicieuse à vivre!

Paul, 23 ans

Mets une croix ⊠ dans la case correcte.

Exemple: Paul aime voyager pour…

☒	**A**	ouvrir de nouveaux horizons
☐	**B**	perfectionner ses compétences linguistiques
☐	**C**	se faire de nouveaux amis
☐	**D**	rendre visite à ses copains

(i) Paul…

☐	**A**	est rentré des vacances récemment
☐	**B**	va passer ses vacances à Montréal
☐	**C**	est de nationalité française
☐	**D**	habite aux États-Unis

(ii) À Montréal…

☐	**A**	il n'y a pas beaucoup de touristes
☐	**B**	on ne se tutoie jamais
☐	**C**	les touristes ne se perdent pas
☐	**D**	on est toujours prêt à aider les touristes

(iii) À Montréal…

☐	**A**	il fait toujours chaud
☐	**B**	il n'y a pas de métro
☐	**C**	les habitants sont plutôt polis
☐	**D**	les gens sont souvent pessimistes

(iv) Au centre de Montréal…

☐	**A**	les transports en commun sont bien développés
☐	**B**	il y a beaucoup de circulation
☐	**C**	la vie est parfaite
☐	**D**	les véhicules sont interdits

(v) Paul…

☐	**A**	préférerait vivre en France
☐	**B**	aime bien vivre à Montréal
☐	**C**	voudrait voyager plus
☐	**D**	trouve les habitants de Montréal assez sympa

(Total for Question 8 = 5 marks)

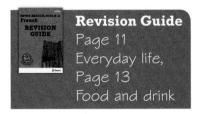

Revision Guide
Page 11
Everyday life,
Page 13
Food and drink

Reading skills

Don't be fazed by longer, more complex passages. Remember that the questions follow the order of the text, so you should be able to work out where you will find the answers.

Vocab hint

Don't panic if you don't know a key word. You can often work out what it means by reading the rest of the text. For example, if you don't know **le surpoids**, first think about the rest of the text, which includes **santé publique** and **obèse**. Then think about how you could break down the word itself into **sur** and **poids**.

 La guerre contre le surpoids

9   Lis cette page web.

> En Guadeloupe, le surpoids est un vrai problème de santé publique vu qu'une personne sur deux est obèse, un chiffre qui est quatre fois plus élevé qu'en France. Le problème va toujours croissant, donc l'Agence régionale de santé (ARS) a déjà lancé de multiples initiatives afin de lutter contre ce fléau. Parmi elles, le programme nutrition-santé Carambole a pour but la prévention contre le surpoids en ciblant les élèves de maternelle.
>
> En essayant de sensibiliser les très jeunes enfants, on veut établir des routines alimentaires plus saines chez une génération d'enfants pour pouvoir réduire le risque de diabète et de problèmes de cœur.
>
> Si la majeure partie des projets de prévention et de sensibilisation concerne les jeunes, il est également nécessaire de ne pas négliger les adultes. Les femmes tout particulièrement qui, en tant que mères, peuvent être les actrices primordiales d'une alimentation saine et équilibrée.

Réponds aux questions **en français**. Il n'est pas nécessaire d'écrire des phrases complètes.

(a) Comment sait-on que l'obésité est un véritable problème en Guadeloupe?

.... **(1 mark)**

(b) Le programme nutrition-santé Carambole concerne qui en particulier?

.... **(1 mark)**

(c) On essaie d'améliorer la santé des jeunes enfants en réduisant quelles **deux** maladies?

....

.... **(2 marks)**

(d) Pourquoi est-ce que les femmes sont particulièrement importantes?

....

.... **(1 mark)**

(Total for Question 9 = 5 marks)

SECTION C

 Translation

10 Translate this passage **into English**.

> Selon mes parents, je suis paresseux et ils disent que je ne fais rien à l'école. Hier soir, ils ont refusé de me laisser sortir avec mes amis car je n'avais pas fini mes devoirs. J'étais vraiment déçu. Je vais essayer d'obtenir de meilleures notes parce que je voudrais avoir plus de liberté à l'avenir.

....
....
....
....
....
....
....
....
....

(Total for Question 10 = 7 marks)

TOTAL FOR PAPER = 50 MARKS

Revision Guide
Page 19
Arranging to go out, Page 52
School life

Translation skills

Check the tenses of the verbs and make sure that you translate them correctly into English.

suis / disent = present

ont refusé = perfect

avais fini = pluperfect

étais = imperfect

vais essayer = near future

voudrais = conditional

Make sure you read through your answer when you have finished, ensuring that it makes sense in English.

Revision Guide
Page 3
Describing family

Hint

If you think that you can develop one bullet point in more detail than the others that is fine. In the sample answer (see the answers section), the first bullet point is more developed as it is a more familiar topic for this student.

Set A Writing Higher practice paper
Time: 1 hour 20 minutes

Total marks: 60
Choose either Question 1(a) or Question 1(b)

Ma famille

1   (a) Alex, ton ami(e) français(e), t'a envoyé un e-mail sur la vie en famille.

Écris une réponse à Alex. Tu **dois** faire référence aux points suivants:

- les membres de ta famille
- tes rapports avec eux
- une visite récente avec ta famille
- vos projets en famille pour le week-end prochain.

Écris 80–90 mots environ **en français**.

....
....
....
....
....
....
....
....
....
....
....
....
....
....
....
....
....
....
....

(Total for Question 1(a) = 20 marks)

L'environnement

(b) Un site Internet français pour les jeunes cherche ton opinion sur
l'environnement.

Écris à ce site Internet. Tu **dois** faire référence aux points suivants:

- le problème environnemental le plus grave selon toi

- ton opinion sur les problèmes environnementaux

- ce que tu as fait récemment pour protéger l'environnement

- tes actions environnementales à l'avenir.

Écris 80–90 mots environ **en français**.

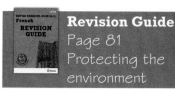

Revision Guide
Page 81
Protecting the
environment

Hint

Make sure that you
understand what the
four bullet points are
asking you to write
about. If you are
not sure, consider
answering the
alternative question
instead. Content marks
very much depend on
how you respond to
the bullet points.

....
....
....
....
....
....
....
....
....
....
....
....
....
....
....
....
....
....
....
....
....
....
....
....
....

(Total for Question 1(b) = 20 marks)

Revision Guide
Page 62
Exchanges

Writing skills

To show off what you know, it is always worth trying to include constructions which use the infinitive in French. Verbs such as *décider de* or *réussir à* + the infinitive and expressions such as *avant de* + the infinitive are impressive when they are used correctly. It is also a good idea to vary your use of common verbs. Have a look at the sample answer in the answer section for examples of how to do this.

Choose either question 2(a) or 2(b)

Une visite scolaire

2   (a)   Vous voulez participer à une visite scolaire dans un collège en France, mais il y a très peu de places disponibles.

Écrivez une lettre pour convaincre le principal de vous offrir une place.

Vous **devez** faire référence aux points suivants:

- pourquoi vous voulez participer
- une visite scolaire récente
- comment la visite va vous aider à l'avenir
- l'importance des langues dans le monde.

Justifiez vos idées et vos opinions.

Écrivez 130–150 mots environ **en français**.

Madame/Monsieur,

....
....
....
....
....
....
....
....
....
....
....
....
....
....
....
....
....

Cordialement

....

(Total for Question 2(a) = 28 marks)

Everyday life

(b) Un magazine français cherche des articles sur la vie des ados pour son site Internet.

Écrivez un article sur votre vie d'adolescent.

Vous **devez** faire référence aux points suivants:

- vos passe-temps préférés et pourquoi vous avez ces passe-temps

- un événement récent mémorable de votre vie

- un nouveau passe-temps que vous aimeriez essayer

- l'importance du temps libre.

Justifiez vos idées et vos opinions.

Écrivez 130–150 mots environ **en français**.

....
....
....
....
....
....
....
....
....
....
....
....
....
....
....
....
....
....
....
....
....
....
....

(Total for Question 2(b) = 28 marks)

Revision Guide
Page 11 Everyday life, Page 16 Social media, Page 20 Hobbies, Page 21 Music, Page 22 Sport

Writing skills

Using pronouns is a good way to raise your language level. Try using *eux / elles*, *me* or *y*, but make sure you put them in the correct place in the sentence. Once you have written your answer, check the sample answer in the answer section for more ideas.

Hint

Although what you write does not necessarily have to be true and you can be creative, what you include should be credible.

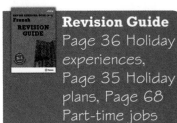

Revision Guide
Page 36 Holiday experiences, Page 35 Holiday plans, Page 68 Part-time jobs

Hint

'Usually', in French, will come either at the start of the sentence or after the verb.

For 'by the sea', you could say 'at the seaside' if you prefer.

Remember, you use **faire** rather than **aller** for shopping. Make sure you use the plural verb.

Think about word order for 'next summer'.

You need to use part of **devoir** for 'I will have to'.

Translation skills

- Consider each verb and decide which tense to use.
- Read the whole text first then work at sentence level to try to produce a French equivalent. As you do this, you can make a checklist:
  verbs: agreement / tense / position in sentence
  nouns: gender / singular/plural
  adjectives: agreement / position
- Check your work thoroughly.

Translation

3   Traduis le passage suivant **en français**:

> I usually spend my holidays in Scotland with my family. Last year I stayed in an enormous hotel by the sea. Every afternoon my parents went shopping while I relaxed on the beach. Next summer I would like to visit Italy with my friends; I will have to earn some money, so I intend to get a part-time job.

....
....
....
....
....
....
....
....
....
....
....
....
....
....
....
....
....
....
....
....
....
....

(Total for Question 3 = 12 marks)

TOTAL FOR PAPER = 60 MARKS

Set B Listening Foundation practice paper

Time: 30 minutes and 5 minutes' reading time

Total marks: 50

SECTION A

Questions and answers in **English**

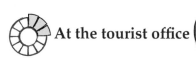At the tourist office

1   What do these people want to do?

Listen to the recording and put a cross ⊠ in each one of the **three** correct boxes.

Example	visit the swimming pool	☒
A	visit the church	☐
B	go cycling	☐
C	go shopping	☐
D	visit a theme park	☐
E	visit the museum	☐
F	find a campsite	☐
G	watch a film	☐

(**Total for Question 1 = 3 marks**)

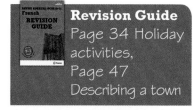

Revision Guide
Page 34 Holiday activities,
Page 47 Describing a town

Listening skills

You often need to listen for the key words. In the example, *faire de la natation* is the French for 'to go swimming'.

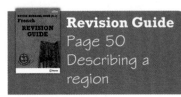

Revision Guide
Page 50
Describing a region

Vocab hint

ne…rien nothing
ne…pas not
seulement only
assez quite

Hint

Make sure you listen to the most important words. You may hear the word for 'large', but what is the **key** word you need?

Hint

Listen carefully for negatives, which can completely change the meaning of a sentence.

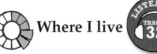 Where I live Listen to the recording

2 Your exchange partner, Hannah, is talking about where she lives.

What does she say?

Listen to the recording and complete these statements by putting a cross ⊠ in the correct box for each question.

Example: Hannah lives…

☒	A	in the countryside
☐	B	in the town centre
☐	C	in the mountains
☐	D	at the seaside

(i) She lives…

☐	A	in quite a small house
☐	B	on a farm
☐	C	in a large flat
☐	D	in a large house

(ii) She doesn't like where she lives because…

☐	A	there is a lot of traffic
☐	B	she has no friends
☐	C	there is nothing to do
☐	D	the weather is bad

(iii) Where she lives…

☐	A	there is a shopping centre
☐	B	there is a supermarket
☐	C	there are no shops
☐	D	there are two shops

(Total for Question 2 = 3 marks)

A French school

Listen to the recording

Revision Guide
Page 52
School life

3   Your exchange partner and her friends are talking about school.

What do they say?

Listen to the recording and put a cross ⊠ next to each one of the **three** correct statements.

		Sophie	Jamel	Rashida
Example	I hate maths	☒	☐	☐
A	I want to use my mobile in class	☐	☐	☐
B	School is boring	☐	☐	☐
C	School is well equipped	☐	☐	☐
D	I get too much homework	☐	☐	☐
E	I play for a school team	☐	☐	☐
F	I want to wear jewellery	☐	☐	☐
G	I don't like the canteen	☐	☐	☐

(Total for Question 3 = 3 marks)

 Part-time jobs

Listen to the recording

4   Your exchange partner is telling you which part-time jobs his friends **Alice**, **Olivier** and **Chloé** have.

Listen to the recording and put a cross ⊠ in each one of the **three** correct boxes.

		Alice	Olivier	Chloé
Example	works in a supermarket	☒	☐	☐
A	wants a different job	☐	☐	☐
B	likes colleagues	☐	☐	☐
C	job is badly paid	☐	☐	☐
D	job is boring	☐	☐	☐
E	works every evening	☐	☐	☐
F	job is interesting	☐	☐	☐
G	works in a café	☐	☐	☐

(Total for Question 4 = 3 marks)

Hint

Look carefully at the number of statements you will need to select and also the row of names. The people will speak in the order that they appear in the table.

Vocab hint

porter = to carry / to wear

Revision Guide
Page 68
Part-time jobs

Listening skills

You will hear each passage twice. First fill in the answers you definitely know then check your answers and fill in any gaps.

Grammar hint

s'entendre bien avec = to get along with. This is a reflexive verb, so it uses a pronoun.
Je m'entends bien avec ma sœur.
Elle s'entend bien avec ses amies.

Hint

Listen out for negatives as these can change the meaning of the verb.

Revision Guide
Page 63
Future plans

 Ambitions

Listen to the recording

5   Your French friend is telling you about her ambitions for the future.
    Listen to the recording and answer the questions **in English**.

    (a) What does she plan to do when she leaves school?

    .... **(1 mark)**

    (b) Where does she plan to travel in the future?

    .... **(1 mark)**

    (c) What type of job would she like?

    .... **(1 mark)**

    (d) What does she say about future relationships?

    .... **(1 mark)**

                                    (Total for Question 5 = 4 marks)

Revision Guide
Page 13
Food and drink

 Eating habits

Listen to the recording

6   Sylvie and Louis are talking about what they like to eat.
    What do they like?
    Complete the sentences. Use the correct word from the box.

~~strawberries~~	sweets	fruit	chips
crisps	meat	fish	chocolate

    (a) Sylvie likes eating ....strawberries.......... and .... **(1 mark)**
    (b) Louis likes eating .... and .... **(2 marks)**

                                    (Total for Question 6 = 3 marks)

Free-time activities

7 During an internet link with your exchange school, Karine tells you what she does in her free time.

What does she say she does?

Listen to the recording and put a cross ⊠ in each one of the **three** correct boxes.

Example	plays table tennis	☒
A	goes cycling	☐
B	plays chess	☐
C	reads novels	☐
D	plays volleyball	☐
E	collects stamps	☐
F	goes water skiing	☐
G	goes skiing	☐

(Total for Question 7 = 3 marks)

 Young people and voluntary work

8 You hear this report on voluntary work among young French people.

Listen to the report and answer the following questions **in English**.

(a) Why do most young people do voluntary work?

.... **(1 mark)**

(b) What reason do 10% of those surveyed give for doing voluntary work?

.... **(1 mark)**

(c) What percentage of those surveyed do work to improve their skills?

.... **(1 mark)**

(Total for Question 8 = 3 marks)

Revision Guide
Page 20
Hobbies

Hint

Make sure that you do not count activities which other people like (for example, Karine's brother).

Vocab hint

Remember all the different ways of giving opinions: j'aime, j'adore, je préfère, je déteste, je n'aime pas, ce n'est pas mon truc, ça m'est égal, ça me plaît / déplaît.

Revision Guide
Page 73
Volunteering

Listening skills

Make sure that you don't confuse numbers which sound similar: deux, dix, douze, for example.

Listening skills

Use some of your preparation time to think of vocabulary related to the topic. Here, for example, you might jot down words associated with voluntary work, such as bénévolat, bénévole, aider, etc.

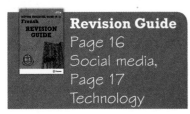

Revision Guide
Page 16
Social media,
Page 17
Technology

Hint

Take care to be exact
in your answers and
listen for the correct
tense of the verb.

Technology   TRACK 39

Listen to the recording

9 You hear this radio programme about internet technology.

Listen to the recording and complete the sentences by putting a
cross ⊠ in the correct box for each question.

Example: Jules goes on social media…

	A	very rarely
	B	once a week
✗	**C**	every day
	D	every weekend

(i) Yesterday Jules…

	A	bought a new mobile
	B	downloaded music online
	C	saw a photo of his family online
	D	lost his mobile

(ii) He uses his computer mostly to…

	A	send emails
	B	research school projects
	C	check sports results
	D	go on forums

(iii) Jules never…

	A	posts photos on sites
	B	uses his real name online
	C	tells anyone his password
	D	lets other people use his computer

(iv) Tomorrow he is going to…

	A	change his password
	B	buy a new tablet
	C	ask his parents for help
	D	contact friends in Scotland

(Total for Question 9 = 4 marks)

Primary school

Listen to the recording

Revision Guide
Page 58
Primary school

10 Your French friend, Lucille, is telling you about her old primary school.

Listen to what she says and answer the questions **in English**.

(a) What did she like best about her primary school?

.... **(1 mark)**

(b) What did she do at break on most days?

.... **(1 mark)**

(c) What does she say about her teachers?

.... **(1 mark)**

(d) What rule did she used to hate?

.... **(1 mark)**

(Total for Question 10 = 4 marks)

Hint

Listen for specific times of day in question (b).

Grammar hint

Remember that the imperfect tense is used to translate the English 'used to' do something. To form this tense for all verbs except **être**, take the **nous** part of the present tense, take off -**ons** and add the imperfect tense endings: -**ais**, -**ais**, -**ait**, -**ions**, -**iez**, -**aient**. For **être**, use j'étais, etc.

Hint

The French often use the 24-hour clock so don't be surprised if you hear numbers above 12 in front of **heures**.

Revision Guide
Page 80
Being green

Hint

Make sure you follow the instructions. You just have to listen for what is mentioned here, but more demanding questions could ask for opinions or differences.

Vocab hint

The vocabulary here is more specialist so make sure you revise this topic in detail.

Revision Guide
Page 39
Holiday problems

Hint

Try not to give too much information if it's not needed. Here, question (b) specifies that you only need to give **one** detail.

Listening skills

Listen for cognates (words which are the same in English and French) or near-cognates (almost the same), for example, agréable, restaurant and impoli.

  Issues in town

11   Your Belgian friend, Marouane, has recorded this message about helping the environment in his home town.

What does he talk about?

Listen to the recording and put a cross ☒ in each one of the **three** correct boxes.

Example	installing more litter bins	☒
A	creating traffic-free zones	☐
B	saving electricity	☐
C	improving public transport	☐
D	reducing noise pollution	☐
E	improving the quality of graffiti	☐
F	creating green belts	☐
G	installing solar panels	☐

(Total for Question 11 = 3 marks)

  A difficult holiday

12   You hear this interview on French radio about a disastrous holiday.

Listen to the interview and answer the following questions **in English**.

(a) How did Salika find the flight to Morocco?

.... **(1 mark)**

(b) What was the problem with the hotel's location? Give **one** detail.

....

.... **(1 mark)**

(c) What does Salika say about the food in the hotel?

.... **(1 mark)**

(d) How is the hotel owner described?

.... **(1 mark)**

(Total for Question 12 = 4 marks)

SECTION B
Questions and answers in French

  Les rapports

Listen to the recording

Revision Guide
Page 3
Describing family

13 Gabriel parle de sa famille.

Complète les phrases en choisissant un mot ou des mots dans la case. Il y a des mots que tu n'utiliseras pas.

son frère aîné	~~sa sœur cadette~~	drôle	énervant
stricte	compréhensive	son petit frère	l'équitation
	le cyclisme	parfois	rarement

Exemple: Louise est ....*sa sœur cadette*..........

(a) Gabriel s'entend mieux avec .... **(1 mark)**

(b) Il trouve Robert .... **(1 mark)**

(c) Il dit que sa mère est très .... **(1 mark)**

(d) Son père aime .... **(1 mark)**

(e) Gabriel fait de la natation .... **(1 mark)**

(Total for Question 13 = 5 marks)

Hint

You won't hear exactly the same words from the box in the recording. Instead, you need to listen out for synonyms (words which mean the same): e.g. petite sœur and sœur cadette.

Hint

Work out which words do not fit or do not make sense and cross them out to rule out some of the alternatives.

Revision Guide
Page 2
Character descriptions

  Mes collègues

Listen to the recording

14 Yolande parle de son travail.

Comment sont ses collègues? Choisis entre: **amusante**, **agaçante**, **gentille** et **généreuse**.

Chacun des mots peut être utilisé plusieurs fois.

Exemple: Nancy est ....*gentille*....

(a) Pauline est très .... **(1 mark)**

(b) Monique n'est pas .... **(1 mark)**

(c) Olivia est toujours .... **(1 mark)**

(d) Connie est vraiment .... **(1 mark)**

(e) Julie est .... **(1 mark)**

(Total for Question 14 = 5 marks)
TOTAL FOR PAPER = 50 MARKS

Listening skills

Look for words that mean the same as the answer options. At this level, you are not likely to hear the same adjectives in the recording. You could jot down what you hear during the first hearing and then see if you can match it to one of the adjectives. For example, if you heard marrante (funny), you would select amusante as the correct answer.

Set B Speaking Foundation practice paper

Time: 19–21 minutes (total), which includes 12 minutes' preparation time

Role play

Topic: Friends and families

Instructions to candidates

You are talking about your family and friends with your French friend. The teacher will play the role of your friend and will speak first.

You must address your French friend as *tu*.

You will talk to the teacher using the five prompts below.

- where you see – **?** – you must ask a question
- where you see – **!** – you must respond to something you have not prepared

Task

> ***Tu parles de la famille et des amis avec ton ami(e) français(e).***
>
> 1. Membre de ta famille – description
> 2. Ta famille – **ton** opinion
> 3. **!**
> 4. Activité préférée avec ta famille
> 5. **?** Meilleur copain

Prepare your answer in this space, using the prompts above. Then play the audio file of the teacher's part and speak your answer in the pauses. You can find a full sample answer of another student's response in the answer section.

Picture-based task

Topic: Future studies

Regarde la photo et prépare des réponses sur les points suivants:

- la description de la photo
- ton opinion sur les avantages d'aller à l'université
- les matières que tu as trouvées utiles au collège
- tes projets pour septembre prochain
- ton opinion sur les apprentissages

Prepare your answer in this space, using the prompts above. Then play the audio file of the teacher's part and speak your answer in the pauses. You can find a full sample answer of another student's response in the answer section.

Revision Guide
Page 52 School life, Page 51 Subjects, Page 63 Future plans, Page 72 Future study

Grammar hint

You can use **on** to mean 'you' in general, but remember that **on** uses the third person singular of the verb (the same as **il / elle**).

Speaking skills

Your teacher can prompt you by asking **Autre chose?** (Is there anything else you want to add?) or **Pourquoi (pas)?** (Why (not)?).

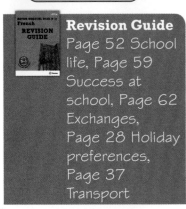

Revision Guide
Page 52 School life, Page 59 Success at school, Page 62 Exchanges, Page 28 Holiday preferences, Page 37 Transport

Speaking skills

Even if a question is asked in the present tense, you can add material which is relevant to the question in a different tense. Take a look at the answers for questions 3 and 4 on page 126 where this has been done: Il y a deux ans, je suis allé...; l'année dernière nous sommes allés...

Speaking skills

You can introduce opinions with phrases like je pense que..., à mon avis..., je préfère.

Grammar hint

The conditional means 'would do something' in English. It's easy to use je voudrais or j'aimerais (I would like) in your conversation.

Hint

Answers which go a bit further allow you to take the initiative in the conversation and are more impressive.

Conversation

Listen to the recording

1 Tu aimes ton école? Pourquoi/pourquoi pas?
2 Qu'est-ce que tu as fait pour profiter de ta scolarité?
3 Que penses-tu des échanges scolaires?
4 Où passes-tu tes vacances normalement?
5 Où aimerais-tu passer tes vacances idéales?
6 C'est quoi, ton moyen de transport préféré? Pourquoi?

Prepare your answer in this space, using the prompts above. Then play the audio file of the teacher's part and speak your answer in the pauses. You can find a full sample answer of another student's response in the answer section.

Set B Reading Foundation practice paper
Time: 45 minutes

Total marks: 50

SECTION A
Questions and answers in **English**

Answer ALL questions. Write your answers in the spaces provided.

Some questions must be answered with a cross in a box ☒. If you change your mind about an answer, put a line through the box ☒ and then mark your new answer with a cross ☒.

 Free-time activities

1 Read these opinions about hobbies on a website.

Jacques:	Je suis très sportif, alors je vais souvent au centre sportif où je joue au volley et au basket. Je préfère les sports d'équipe.
Tammy:	Je déteste le sport. Je préfère faire les magasins ou écouter de la musique chez moi avec mes copines.
Johan:	Ma passion c'est la lecture. Je lis chaque jour mais j'aime aussi regarder la télé. Je préfère la télé-réalité.
Kathy:	Je n'ai pas beaucoup de temps libre parce que j'ai trop de travail scolaire. De temps en temps je vais au ciné.

Who says what about their free-time activities? Enter either **Jacques**, **Tammy**, **Johan** or **Kathy**.

You can use each person more than once.

Example: ......Jacques...... plays volleyball.

(a) .... likes reading.   **(1 mark)**

(b) .... has little free time.   **(1 mark)**

(c) .... sometimes watches a film.   **(1 mark)**

(d) .... likes reality TV shows.   **(1 mark)**

(e) .... likes shopping.   **(1 mark)**

(f) .... prefers team sports.   **(1 mark)**

(Total for Question 1 = 6 marks)

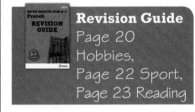

Revision Guide
Page 20 Hobbies,
Page 22 Sport,
Page 23 Reading

Hint

Don't focus too much on individual words in the questions. For example, 'film' does not appear in the text so look for words which might mean the same or activities which are associated with films.

Reading skills

Take care with words which look like English words but have different meanings such as magasins (not magazines) or lecture (not lecture).

Grammar hint

Remember it is jouer à with a sport you would 'play' in English and faire de for other sports. But for instruments, it is jouer de.

Revision Guide
Page 82
Environmental
issues

Grammar hint

Remember that adjectives in French usually agree with the word that they describe so normally add **e** for feminine, **s** for plural and **es** for feminine plural. Look here at **les trajets courts** but note that **bio** is an exception– it never changes its spelling.

Hint

Remember to read texts closely as there can be negatives or other phrases which can lead you to a wrong answer. For example, question (c) refers to short journeys (**trajets courts**) which is in the text, so look back and check if the means of transport mentioned is correct.

 Helping the environment

2 Read the advert below about the ways in which Marco the Mole helps the environment.

Je m'appelle Marco et j'aime protéger la planète. Je prends toujours une douche au lieu d'un bain. Je recycle les journaux tous les jours et je recycle les bouteilles le lundi et le vendredi. Je prends le bus ou, pour les trajets courts, je me déplace à vélo. Quand je vais au supermarché, j'achète des produits bio. J'économise aussi l'électricité.

Complete the gap in each sentence using a word or words from the box below. There are more words than gaps.

bath	shower	glass	home	bus	green
~~planet~~	energy	paper	money	bike	cheap

Example: Marco likes protecting the ....planet............

(a) He never has a .... **(1 mark)**

(b) He recycles .... twice a week. **(1 mark)**

(c) For short journeys he travels by .... **(1 mark)**

(d) He tries to buy products which are .... **(1 mark)**

(e) He also saves .... **(1 mark)**

(Total for Question 2 = 5 marks)

 **Homelessness**

3 (a) Read this article about social problems.

> Selon un sondage récent à Paris, il y a plus de trois mille sans-abri qui dorment dans les rues de la capitale. Naturellement ils n'ont pas d'emploi. Ils reçoivent des pièces de monnaie des passants dans la rue, mais ils ont froid, surtout en hiver, et parfois peur aussi. C'est une situation qui laisse beaucoup à désirer.

Answer the following questions **in English**. You do not need to write in full sentences.

(i) How many homeless people are there in Paris?

.... **(1 mark)**

(ii) Apart from a home, what else do they not have?

.... **(1 mark)**

(iii) At what time of year are their problems especially bad?

.... **(1 mark)**

(b) The article continues.

> La plupart des sans-abri sont jeunes, ils ont moins de trente ans. Il faut encourager le gouvernement à aider ces pauvres car c'est un problème grave. Selon presque tout le monde, il y a trop de sans-abri partout en France.

(i) What does the article say about the majority of the homeless people?

.... **(1 mark)**

(ii) Who should help the homeless, according to the article?

.... **(1 mark)**

(Total for Question 3 = 5 marks)

Revision Guide
Page 74
Helping others

Hint

Make sure that you try to give exact details when numbers are asked for. You can easily confuse some larger numbers, so revise them before the exam.

Vocab hint

Take care with specific vocabulary items. Try to make your own lists to learn and put them into different categories, such as adjectives. Here, you might learn *jeune*.

Hint

Remember to read the questions thoroughly, as they can provide information about the passage as a whole.

Vocab hint

selon un sondage
according to a survey

pièces de monnaie
coins

avoir peur to be afraid

Revision Guide
Page 3
Describing family

Reading skills

This is an authentic French text. Sometimes, some of the language used might be quite unusual, but don't worry if you don't understand it all: you won't need to know it all to answer the questions.

Vocab hint

When you do need to work out the meaning of a word, look at the other words around it to help you. For example, **parapet** may be unknown but it is linked to **y monter** (to go up there), which is the clue you need.

Reading skills

Read the text a couple of times before you start on the questions. You might find that some words later in the passage will help you understand what is happening earlier on.

 Le Rouge et le Noir by Stendhal

4   Read the extract (adapted) from the text below.

A family outing is being described.

> C'était par un beau jour d'automne que M. de Rênal se promenait sur la plage, donnant le bras à sa femme. Tout en écoutant son mari qui parlait d'un air grave, l'oeil de madame de Rênal suivait avec inquiétude les mouvements de leurs trois petits fils. L'aîné, qui pouvait avoir onze ans, s'approchait trop souvent du parapet et essayait d'y monter. Une voix douce prononçait alors le nom d'Adolphe, et l'enfant renonçait à son projet ambitieux. Madame de Rênal paraissait une femme de trente ans, mais encore assez jolie.

(Adapted from *Le Rouge et le Noir*, Stendhal)

Put a cross ⊠ in the correct box.

Example: The outing took place in…

☒	**A**	autumn
☐	**B**	winter
☐	**C**	spring
☐	**D**	summer

(i) The family was…

☐	**A**	in town
☐	**B**	at the seaside
☐	**C**	in a house
☐	**D**	in the mountains

(ii) Mme de Rênal was…

☐	**A**	watching her husband
☐	**B**	speaking to her husband
☐	**C**	listening to her husband
☐	**D**	following her husband

(iii) She seemed…

☐	**A**	happy
☐	**B**	worried
☐	**C**	carefree
☐	**D**	sad

(iv) The eldest son…

☐	**A**	was chasing Adolphe
☐	**B**	was speaking quietly
☐	**C**	was trying to do some climbing
☐	**D**	was about 13 years old

(v) According to the passage Mme de Rênal is…

☐	**A**	about 40 years old
☐	**B**	ambitious
☐	**C**	quite happy
☐	**D**	quite pretty

(Total for Question 4 = 5 marks)

A part-time job

5   Read what Alice says about her part-time job.

> J'ai commencé mon petit boulot dans un magasin de vêtements il
> y a six mois. Je sers les clients et je nettoie le magasin à la fin de
> la journée le samedi et le dimanche. Je m'entends assez bien avec
> le propriétaire et je reçois dix euros par heure. J'ai économisé un
> peu d'argent car je voudrais m'acheter une nouvelle robe pour
> l'anniversaire de ma tante.

Answer the following questions **in English**. You do not need to
write in full sentences.

(a) Where does Alice work?

……………………………………………………………………… **(1 mark)**

(b) What does she do at the end of the days when she works?

……………………………………………………………………… **(1 mark)**

(c) Why has she been saving up her money?

……………………………………………………………………… **(1 mark)**

(Total for Question 5 = 3 marks)

Revision Guide
Page 68
Part-time jobs

Hint

Remember that the
questions follow the
order of the text. There
might be sentences in
the text which don't
provide any answers,
but they might still help
you to establish the
context.

Revision Guide
Page 73
Volunteering

Hint

Remember to give exact answers. For example, question (b) needs a detailed response here.

Vocab hint

Try to use your common sense to help guess unknown vocabulary. For example, **décorer** and **Noël** could help with the meaning of **sapin**.

 Volunteering

6   Read Delphine's blog about her favourite celebration.

> Noël me plaît bien et c'est sans doute ma fête préférée. J'adore surtout décorer le sapin de Noël et j'aime donner et recevoir des cadeaux, bien sûr. L'an dernier, je suis allé à un grand marché de Noël à Colmar et j'y ai acheté une montre en or comme cadeau pour mon petit ami.
>
> La veille de Noël, toute la famille se réunit normalement chez mon oncle où on mange un énorme repas avant d'aller à la messe de minuit. L'année prochaine tout va changer: on a décidé de passer Noël chez ma sœur aînée parce qu'elle va bientôt acheter sa propre maison.

Answer the questions **in English**. You do not need to write in full sentences.

(a)   What does Delphine particularly enjoy doing at Christmas?

.... **(1 mark)**

(b)   What exactly did she buy in Colmar for her boyfriend?

.... **(1 mark)**

(c)   What does the family usually do before church on Christmas Eve?

....

.... **(1 mark)**

(d)   What will change next Christmas?

....

.... **(1 mark)**

(Total for Question 6 = 4 marks)

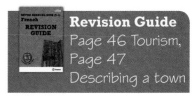
Revision Guide
Page 46 Tourism,
Page 47
Describing a town

SECTION B
Questions and answers in **French**

 **Le tourisme**

7 Lis ces descriptions sur un site Internet touristique.

Rouen:	Festival international de musique. Entrée gratuite du 11 au 14 août.
Lyon:	Festival d'art contemporain au musée Gaillard du 1er au 30 juin. Entrée 5 euros, réductions pour les groupes.
Nancy:	Festival de l'humour. Sketchs et blagues tous les soirs du 15 au 20 juillet 12 euros.
Biarritz:	Démonstrations de planche à voile du 4 au 7 septembre à partir de 11h. Location de planches 20 euros.

Quelle est la ville correcte? Choisis entre: **Rouen, Lyon, Nancy** et **Biarritz**.

Chacun des mots peut être utilisé plusieurs fois.

Exemple: On peut participer à un festival de musique à ....*Rouen*.....

(a) On peut faire un sport nautique à .... **(1 mark)**

(b) Il ne faut pas payer à .... **(1 mark)**

(c) On va certainement rire à .... **(1 mark)**

(d) On peut regarder des peintures à .... **(1 mark)**

(e) On peut louer un équipement à .... **(1 mark)**

(Total for Question 7 = 5 marks)

Hint

In questions like this, the sentences do not come in the order of the text, so make sure you look back at the text as a whole.

Hint

Take care with false friends such as location – it does not mean 'location' in English.

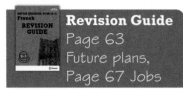

Revision Guide
Page 63
Future plans,
Page 67 Jobs

Hint

Don't just assume that if the words in the answer options also appear in the text, that that answer must be correct. You may need to look for a negative or a synonym (e.g. *ce n'est pas un travail bien payé*).

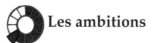 Les ambitions

8   Lis ces opinions sur des projets pour le futur.

Marianne:	Moi, je vais trouver un emploi comme infirmière parce que j'aimerais aider les autres. Je sais que ce n'est pas un travail bien payé, mais pour moi ce qui importe, c'est d'être heureux.
Paulette:	Après avoir fini mes études universitaires, je voudrais voyager un peu afin de découvrir d'autres pays et d'élargir mes horizons. Je ne veux pas faire comme ma mère qui s'est mariée à l'âge de dix-sept ans et qui a eu trois enfants avant d'avoir vingt-et-un ans. Je veux être plus libre.
Sylvia:	Je ne sais pas ce que je vais faire à l'avenir. Je suis trop jeune pour décider définitivement mon futur. On me dit de suivre mes rêves, mais j'en ai beaucoup!

Mets une croix ⊠ dans la case correcte.

Exemple: Marianne veut devenir…

☒	**A**	infirmière
☐	**B**	médecin
☐	**C**	actrice
☐	**D**	informaticienne

(i) Marianne…

☐	**A**	voudrait être riche
☐	**B**	aimerait être contente
☐	**C**	voudrait voyager
☐	**D**	aimerait un emploi bien payé

(ii) Paulette va aller…

☐	**A**	aux États-Unis
☐	**B**	en Espagne
☐	**C**	à l'université
☐	**D**	faire du ski

(iii) Elle ne va pas…

☐	**A**	voyager beaucoup
☐	**B**	découvrir d'autres pays
☐	**C**	faire comme sa mère
☐	**D**	goûter d'autres cultures

(iv) Elle voudrait…

☐	**A**	se marier avant l'âge de 21 ans
☐	**B**	avoir trois enfants
☐	**C**	suivre l'exemple de sa mère
☐	**D**	avoir plus de liberté

(v) Sylvia…

☐	**A**	sait ce qu'elle va faire à l'avenir
☐	**B**	est très âgée
☐	**C**	a plein de rêves
☐	**D**	va suivre les conseils de ses copains

(Total for Question 8 = 5 marks)

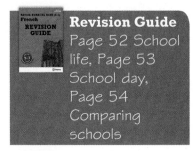

Revision Guide
Page 52 School life, Page 53 School day, Page 54 Comparing schools

Hint

Work out the meaning of the sentences before you try to fill the gaps and use your grammatical knowledge to eliminate possible answers. For example, the answer to (e) follows **faire** so must start with **de**.

 Une école différente

9   Lis cet e-mail d'Amadou.

> J'habite au Sénégal et mon collège est très grand car il y a plus de deux mille élèves. On commence très tôt, à six heures et demie, et les cours finissent à quatorze heures. Je vais au collège à vélo. Dans ma classe d'anglais nous sommes quarante et tous les élèves pensent qu'apprendre au moins deux langues est vraiment important. Nous n'avons pas beaucoup d'installations mais un lycée en France nous a donné plusieurs ordinateurs et je trouve ça génial. Nous avons un terrain de sport où on fait du sport, surtout du foot. Malheureusement il n'y a pas de piscine.

Complète chaque phrase en utilisant un mot de la case. Attention! Il y a des mots que tu n'utiliseras pas.

~~Sénégal~~	de natation	français	les élèves
informatique	le rugby	de bonne heure	les sportifs
du cyclisme	tard	le foot	France

Exemple: Amadou habite au .....Sénégal.....

(a) Au collège d'Amadou, les cours commencent.......................

     ....   **(1 mark)**

(b) .... croient qu'il est important d'étudier
     les langues.   **(1 mark)**

(c) Une école française a donné du matériel pour les cours

     d'..............................   **(1 mark)**

(d) Au collège, le sport principal est .... **(1 mark)**

(e) Au collège, on ne peut pas faire .... **(1 mark)**

     (Total for Question 9 = 5 marks)

SECTION C

 Translation

10 Translate this passage **into English**.

> J'aime aller en vacances. D'habitude je vais en Angleterre avec mes parents. Nous faisons du camping parce que nous aimons le plein air. L'année dernière je suis allé au bord de la mer en Écosse. C'était formidable mais il a fait assez froid.

....

....

....

....

....

....

....

....

....

(Total for Question 10 = 7 marks)

TOTAL FOR PAPER = 50 MARKS

**Set B
Reading**
Foundation

 Revision Guide
Page 28 Holiday preferences,
Page 32 Holiday destinations

Translation skills

Translate carefully, sentence by sentence. You need to translate every word, but that doesn't always mean writing down the English equivalent of each French word one by one. Sometimes French uses different word order or words have different meanings, depending on the sentence.

Hint

Take care with tenses. Look at je suis allé, il a fait and c'était and remember that they all refer to l'année dernière.

Hint

In the first sentence en will not mean 'in' here, so be careful.

Faisons is part of faire but it won't be translated as 'do' here.

Remember, nous = we.

Don't forget to translate little words like assez.

Make sure that you don't write something in English which does not make sense, e.g. 'we make camping'.

Set B Writing Foundation practice paper
Time: 1 hour 10 minutes

Total marks: 60

Un tournoi sportif

Revision Guide
Page 22 Sport

1   Tu participes à un tournoi sportif en Belgique. Tu postes cette photo sur des médias sociaux pour tes amis.

Écris une description de la photo **et** exprime ton opinion sur le sport.

Écris 20–30 mots environ **en français**.

....

....

....

....

....

....

....

....

....

....

(Total for Question 1 = 12 marks)

Writing skills

Keep your answer quite simple as there are only marks for communication here. There is no need to extend your answers.

Hint

Make sure you give an opinion when you are asked to.

Un festival de musique

2 Vous allez participer à un festival de musique en Suisse. Vous écrivez au directeur du festival où vous allez.

Revision Guide
Page 79
Music events

Écrivez un e-mail avec les informations suivantes:

- votre instrument de musique préféré

- ce que vous allez faire au festival

- la musique que vous aimez

- pourquoi vous voulez aller en Suisse.

Il faut écrire en phrases complètes.

Écrivez 40–50 mots environ **en français**.

Madame/Monsieur,

....

....

....

....

....

....

....

....

....

....

....

....

....

....

Cordialement

....

(Total for Question 2 = 16 marks)

Grammar hint

Remember that 'to play' a musical instrument is *jouer de...*

Writing skills

You will not need to develop your answers much as there is not much room for this in 40 words but make sure that you cover all four bullet points. You could start to link sentences using *parce que*, *mais*, *et* and *car* as this will be useful for later tasks in the exam.

Revision Guide
Page 52
School life

Writing skills

Try to vary the connectives you use. Remember that car, parce que and puisque are all possible ways of explaining an opinion.

Hint

You will need to develop your answer and also refer to three time frames in response to the four bullet points. You do not have to write exactly the same amount on each bullet point, but you must cover all four.

Mon école

Choose either Question 3(a) or Question 3(b)

3 (a) Dominique, ton ami(e) français(e), veut savoir comment tu trouves l'école.

Écris une réponse à Dominique. Tu **dois** faire référence aux points suivants:

- ton opinion sur ton école
- ce que tu as fait récemment au collège
- ta matière préférée et pourquoi.
- tes projets d'études pour l'avenir.

Écris 80–90 mots environ **en français**.

....
....
....
....
....
....
....
....
....
....
....
....
....
....
....
....
....
....
....
....
....
....

(Total for Question 3(a) = 20 marks)

Les vacances

(b) Un site français pour les jeunes cherche ton opinion sur les vacances.

Écris un article pour ce site Internet.

Tu **dois** faire référence aux points suivants:

- ce que tu aimes faire en vacances
- où tu as passé tes vacances l'année dernière
- pourquoi les vacances sont importantes ou non
- tes projets de vacances pour l'année prochaine.

Écris 80–90 mots environ **en français**.

Revision Guide
Page 28 Holiday
preferences

Grammar hint

Remember that some verbs of motion such as **aller**, **arriver** and **sortir** use **être** as the auxiliary verb in the perfect tense and that the past participle must agree with the subject of the verb in these cases. Bear this in mind when responding to the second bullet point (**je suis allé(e)** (I went), etc.). See pages 100 and 101 of the Revision Guide for more on the perfect tense.

....

....

....

....

....

....

....

....

....

....

....

....

....

....

....

....

....

....

....

....

....

....

....

....

(Total for Question 3(b) = 20 marks)

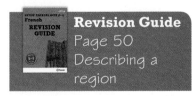

Revision Guide
Page 50
Describing a
region

Hint

Which one of **mon**, **ma** or **mes** do you need for 'my' in sentence (a)?

For sentence (b) remember what follows 'lots' in French.

In sentence (d) 'visiting' will be translated by 'to visit' in French. Remember that the French say '**the** museums' and 'never' = **ne...jamais**.

Remember to use the correct tense for 'went' and 'bought' in sentence (e).

Ma région

4   Traduis les phrases suivantes **en français**.

(a) I like my town.

.... **(2 marks)**

(b) There are lots of shops.

.... **(2 marks)**

(c) The sports centre in town is new.

.... **(2 marks)**

(d) I never like visiting museums.

....

.... **(3 marks)**

(e) Yesterday I went to the castle where I bought a gift for my brother.

....

.... **(3 marks)**

(Total for Question 4 = 12 marks)

TOTAL FOR PAPER = 60 MARKS

Set B Listening Higher practice paper

Time: 40 minutes and 5 minutes' reading time

Total marks: 50

SECTION A

Questions and answers in **French**

 **Ma ville**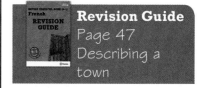

Listen to the recording

1 Florence parle de sa ville.

Complète les phrases en choisissant un mot ou des mots dans la case. Il y a des mots que tu n'utiliseras pas.

jeunes	zones piétonnes	~~un village~~	propre
une ferme	beaucoup de chose	magasins	nuls
circulation	rien	assez bons	sale

Exemple: Florence habitait dans .... un village ....

(a) Sa ville est .... **(1 mark)**

(b) Il y a quelques .... fermés au
centre-ville. **(1 mark)**

(c) Il n'y a pas .... pour les jeunes
en ville. **(1 mark)**

(d) Florence trouve les transports en commun

.... **(1 mark)**

(e) Comme problème, il y a beaucoup de

.... en ville. **(1 mark)**

(Total for Question 1 = 5 marks)

Revision Guide
Page 47
Describing a town

Hint

Make time in your preparation period to work out what each of the answer options means.

Hint

Look out for negatives as they can change the meaning of sentences.

Grammar hint

Take care to check that any adjectives agree with the noun they describe. For example, if the noun is plural, the adjective will probably end in an -s, so you can discount any answer options which don't.

Revision Guide
Page 24 Films

Hint

Always check instructions to make sure that you are doing what has been asked. For example, here it says that the adjectives can be used several times.

Hint

When deciding between **intéressant** (interesting) and **passionnant** (exciting), try listening for words which have the same or similar meanings as these.

 **Les films**

Listen to the recording

2   André parle des films.

Que pense-t-il de chaque film? Choisis entre: **intéressant**, **passionnant**, **nul** et **marrant**.

Chacun des mots peut être utilisé plusieurs fois.

Exemple: Selon André, le documentaire était ....intéressant........

(a) Le film de guerre était .... **(1 mark)**

(b) André a trouvé le dessin animé .... **(1 mark)**

(c) Selon André, le film d'action était .... **(1 mark)**

(d) Il a trouvé le film d'espionnage .... **(1 mark)**

(e) Le film de science-fiction était .... **(1 mark)**

(Total for Question 2 = 5 marks)

SECTION B
Questions and answers in **English**

 Christmas celebrations

3 Your exchange partner's friends are talking about Christmas.

Listen to the recording and complete the sentences by putting a cross ⊠ in the correct box for each question.

Revision Guide
Page 26
Celebrations

Example: Alice used to spend Christmas…

☐	**A**	with friends
☐	**B**	with her grandparents
☐	**C**	with her mum
☒	**D**	with her family

Listening skills

At Higher tier you will often be asked to listen for more than one answer in each extract. Make sure you keep concentrating right to the end of each section.

(i) Alice spends Christmas Eve…

☐	**A**	with her mother
☐	**B**	with her father
☐	**C**	with both her parents
☐	**D**	with her friends

(ii) She is…

☐	**A**	always happy at Christmas
☐	**B**	fed up because she doesn't get enough presents
☐	**C**	sad even though she gets lots of presents
☐	**D**	really pleased as she gets lots of presents

(iii) Yannick used to…

☐	**A**	look forward to Christmas
☐	**B**	go to a shopping centre to buy presents
☐	**C**	attend a church service
☐	**D**	find Christmas too commercialised

(iv) Yannick doesn't like…

☐	**A**	getting presents associated with technology
☐	**B**	the fact that people always want the latest models of technology devices
☐	**C**	not seeing his friends at Christmas
☐	**D**	not getting the presents he wants at Christmas

(Total for Question 3 = 4 marks)

Revision Guide
Page 82
Environmental issues

Listening skills

In questions where there is more than one speaker, make sure that you don't get confused about who says what. For example, the answers D and G seem to contradict each other, so they are probably not both correct!

Hint

Remember that in this type of activity, it can help to cross off items that you know are not true to help you focus your attention on the possible correct answers.

Vocab hint

If you hear a word you don't know, think around the problem. For example, if you have forgotten or do not know **le déboisement**, consider whether you recognise the stem of the word: **bois**. Putting **de** on the front of the word often means 'to reverse' or 'to remove' (as in English): e.g. **déconstruire, détacher.**

Environmental issues

Listen to the recording

4   Your exchange partner, Pauline, is discussing the environment with her brother.

What do they say?

Listen to the recording and put a cross ⊠ in each one of the **three** correct boxes.

Example	Pauline is concerned about animals threatened with extinction	☒
A	Pauline thinks that people are selfish	☐
B	Pauline believes that lots has been done to help animals in danger	☐
C	Pauline's brother mentions droughts in some countries	☐
D	Pauline's brother believes that flooding is the biggest environmental issue	☐
E	Pauline mentions islands which are under threat	☐
F	Pauline mentions deforestation	☐
G	Pauline's brother is not concerned about rising sea levels	☐

(Total for Question 4 = 3 marks)

 Le camping

Revision Guide
Page 30
Campsites

5 Your French friend, Annick, is describing her holiday.

Listen to the recording and put a cross ☒ in the correct box for each question.

Example: Annick likes going on holiday…

☐	**A**	once a month
☒	**B**	at least twice a year
☐	**C**	once a year
☐	**D**	only in summer

(i) She really liked…

☐	**A**	the weather
☐	**B**	being in Britain
☐	**C**	the outdoor pool
☐	**D**	the playground

(ii) She found the showers…

☐	**A**	sometimes too hot
☐	**B**	always cold
☐	**C**	sometimes cold
☐	**D**	just right

(iii) On holiday Annick likes…

☐	**A**	going camping
☐	**B**	staying with her family
☐	**C**	a bit of luxury
☐	**D**	being active

(Total for Question 5 = 3 marks)

Revision Guide
Page 51
Subjects

Hint

At Higher tier, the answer to the question is not always obvious. Read the questions before the recording starts so you know roughly what to expect.

Then listen to the sense of the whole section of the recording. Write brief notes if you hear the answer to the question so that you can keep listening.

Don't worry if you don't hear an exact translation of what is said in the question – remember that at Higher tier you often have to work out what is meant.

 Choosing subjects

6   You hear your Swiss friends discussing the subjects they chose to study.

Listen to the conversation and answer these questions **in English**.

(a) Why did Julie choose English?

.... **(1 mark)**

(b) Why has her decision been a good one?

.... **(1 mark)**

(c) Why did Manon choose physics?

....

.... **(1 mark)**

(d) Why has this turned out badly for her?

.... **(1 mark)**

(e) Why was Lopez considering studying Portuguese? Give **two** details.

....

.... **(2 marks)**

(Total for Question 6 = 6 marks)

 Holidays

Listen to the recording

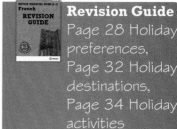

Revision Guide
Page 28 Holiday preferences,
Page 32 Holiday destinations,
Page 34 Holiday activities

7 You hear this interview with Marcel Dumoulin of the Quebec tourist board on the radio.

Listen to the interview and answer the following questions **in English**.

(a) What did 80% of the people surveyed say about holidays?

.... **(1 mark)**

(b) What was the most popular holiday activity mentioned?

.... **(1 mark)**

(c) What type of destination was the favourite, according to the survey?

.... **(1 mark)**

(d) Which destination has lost popularity?

.... **(1 mark)**

(Total for Question 7 = 4 marks)

Hint

Be careful to listen to the context. Several typical holiday activities are mentioned but you need to listen for the most popular one.

  Social networks

Listen to the recording

8 You hear a news programme about problems with social network sites.

Listen to the recording and put a cross ☒ in the correct box for each question.

Example: The man usually…

☐	**A**	prefers to stay at home during the holidays
☒	**B**	keeps his friends informed about where he is going on holiday
☐	**C**	never contacts his friends during his holidays
☐	**D**	likes to go on holiday abroad

Revision Guide
Page 16
Social media

Hint

With topics such as social media, don't allow your own experiences to affect what you hear. Make sure your answers reflect what you hear on the recording.

Part (a)

(i) In the future, the man…

☐	**A**	will post a message about his holiday online
☐	**B**	will never book his holidays online
☐	**C**	will not post holiday photos online
☐	**D**	will never reveal online that he is going on holiday

Grammar hint

Object pronouns

Me (me), te / vous (you), nous (us), le (him / it), la (her / it) and les (them) are common **direct object pronouns**. In the perfect tense, they come **before the auxiliary verb**. In this case, the past participle **needs to agree** with the preceding direct object. Remember that le and la will change to l'.

je l'ai vu I saw him

je l'ai vue I saw her

je les ai vu(e)s I saw them

Me (to me), te / vous (to you), nous (to us), lui (to him / her / it) and leur (to them) are **indirect object pronouns**.

They go in the same position as direct object pronouns, but the past participle **does not agree** with them.

je lui ai donné de l'argent I gave some money to him / her

(ii) The man lost…

☐	**A**	all his possessions
☐	**B**	details of his log-in
☐	**C**	his money when his holiday was cancelled
☐	**D**	everything he had saved online

Part (b)

(i) The woman was silly…

☐	**A**	to discuss animal testing online
☐	**B**	to criticise her boss online
☐	**C**	to advertise a watch online
☐	**D**	to post photos online

(ii) She…

☐	**A**	sent inappropriate emails
☐	**B**	advertised tickets for shows
☐	**C**	lost her job
☐	**D**	helped someone find a new job

Part (c)

(i) The boy…

☐	**A**	makes friends easily
☐	**B**	rarely uses the internet
☐	**C**	comes from a big family
☐	**D**	has no siblings

(ii) The boy…

☐	**A**	has lots of friends
☐	**B**	hopes to make friends online
☐	**C**	is going to subscribe to a new social network site
☐	**D**	wants to learn how to best use the internet

(Total for Question 8 = 6 marks)

  Weather problems

9 You are listening to a report about weather problems in Mauritius on French radio.

Answer the following questions **in English**.

Part (a)

(i) What is the problem in Mauritius?

.... **(1 mark)**

(ii) For how long has the weather been an issue?

.... **(1 mark)**

(iii) Which towns and villages have been worst affected?

.... **(1 mark)**

(iv) What has happened to some inhabitants?

.... **(1 mark)**

(v) What new risk is there for some inhabitants?

.... **(1 mark)**

(vi) What problem is being faced by aid organisations?

.... **(1 mark)**

Part (b)

(i) How many French holiday-makers are on the island?

.... **(1 mark)**

(ii) What will the French government try to do?

.... **(1 mark)**

(iii) What has it already done? Give **two** details.

....

.... **(2 marks)**

(Total for Question 9 = 10 marks)

Revision Guide
Page 45
Weather

Hint

Be exact – remember that little words like presque can be important.

Vocab hint

At this level, you might hear unfamiliar vocabulary. Don't panic, but try to work out what it means from everything else you are told.

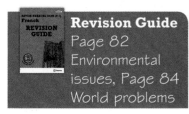

Revision Guide
Page 82
Environmental
issues, Page 84
World problems

Vocab hint

Be careful when you are listening to more complex passages. You might hear a word, such as **course** or **occasion**, which has more than one meaning, so remember to consider both meanings.

Hint

Listen to the tenses of verbs and make sure that they are the same in both the French recording and the English answer options.

Vocab hint

Listen for words you **do** know to try to help with the meaning of words you **don't** know. For example, you might recognise **vente** so you could work out what **vente d'occasion** means.

Hint

Sometimes what is **not** said can help you to pin down meanings. Listen for time phrases: is the sale happening in a few weeks' time?

 Être solidaire

10 Your hear Sophie and Vincent talking about world problems.
Put a cross ⊠ in each one of the **two** correct boxes for each question.

(i) What does Sophie say?

Example	Sophie says that we must respect the environment	☒
A	She is going to adopt a tiger	☐
B	She only buys environmentally friendly products	☐
C	She has helped people with shopping	☐
D	She is worried about world hunger	☐
E	She is going to take part in a demonstration	☐

(2 marks)

(ii) What does Vincent say?

A	He has organised a fundraising activity	☐
B	He hopes to be able to give second-hand clothes to the homeless	☐
C	A sale will take place in a few weeks' time	☐
D	Vincent is proud of the people who have helped him	☐
E	He knows that he can do little to help the poor	☐

(2 marks)

(Total for Question 10 = 4 marks)

TOTAL FOR PAPER = 50 MARKS

Set B Speaking Higher practice paper

Time: 22–24 minutes (total), which includes 12 minutes' preparation time

Role play

Topic: Travel and tourist transactions

Instructions to candidates

You are talking to an employee at a French tourist office. The teacher will play the role of the employee and will speak first.

You should address the employee as *vous*.

You will talk to the teacher using the five prompts below.

- where you see this – ? – you must ask a question
- where you see this – ! – you will have to respond to something you have not prepared

Task

> *Vous parlez avec un(e) employé(e) dans un office du tourisme en France.*
>
> 1. Région – opinion
> 2. !
> 3. Durée des vacances
> 4. ? Les transports en commun
> 5. ? Sports dans la région

Prepare your answer in this space, using the prompts above. Then play the audio file of the teacher's part and speak your answer in the pauses. You can find a full sample answer of another student's response in the answer section.

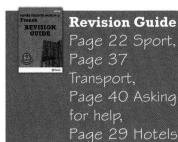

Speaking skills

The role play will last 2–2.5 minutes, the picture-based task will be 3–3.5 minutes and the conversation will last 5–6 minutes.

Revision Guide
Page 22 Sport,
Page 37 Transport,
Page 40 Asking for help,
Page 29 Hotels

Hint

If you are asked for an opinion, be brief. There are no extra marks for giving reasons or adding details in a role play and you might make errors.

Grammar hint

If you are using adjectives, make sure that they agree.

Revision Guide
Page 26
Celebrations

Hint

Don't be put off by tricky-looking questions. Stay focused and find something to say. Try to develop your answers if you can.

Speaking skills

Your teacher can prompt you by asking **Autre chose?** (Is there anything else you want to add?) or **Pourquoi (pas)?** (Why (not)?).

Speaking skills

Try to do as much to prepare for the unexpected question as you can in advance. For example, you know the topic so think of questions which might be asked on that subject. As you will need to give an opinion on a more general aspect of the topic, it might be worth learning some opinions and reasons.

Picture-based task

Topic: Cultural life

Regarde la photo et prépare des réponses sur les points suivants:

- la description de la photo
- ton opinion sur l'importance des fêtes nationales
- un mariage récent
- si tu voudrais te marier un jour
- !

Prepare your answer in this space, using the prompts above. Then play the audio file of the teacher's part and speak your answer in the pauses. You can find a full sample answer of another student's response in the answer section.

Conversation

Listen to the recording

1 Qu'est-ce que tes parents font dans la vie?
2 Quel est ton emploi idéal? Pourquoi?
3 Quel travail est-ce que tu voulais faire quand tu étais plus jeune?
4 Quels sont tes plus grands accomplissements au collège?
5 Que penses-tu des échanges scolaires?
6 Tu fais partie d'un club au collège?

Prepare your answer in this space, using the prompts above. Then play the audio file of the teacher's part and speak your answer in the pauses. You can find a full sample answer of another student's response in the answer section.

Revision Guide
Page 67 Jobs,
Page 7 When
I was younger,
Page 59
Success at
school, Page 62
Exchanges,
Page 52
School life

Hint

Remember that the answers given in the answer section are just samples to give you an idea of what you might say. Obviously, you can use your own opinions and ideas.

Listening skills

You will need to listen carefully to your teacher when he / she asks the question. For example, in question 1, **la vie** is related to 'living', so the question is asking what your parents do for a living.

Hint

Remember to develop your answers when you can. The conversation will require you to speak spontaneously, but you can nominate the first theme, so make sure you choose wisely.

Set B Reading Higher practice paper
Time: 1 hour

Total marks: 50

Answer ALL questions. Write your answers in the spaces provided.

Some questions must be answered with a cross in a box ⊠. If you change your mind about an answer, put a line through the box ⊠ and then mark your new answer with a cross ⊠.

SECTION A
Questions and answers in **English**

 Using the internet

Revision Guide
Page 17
Technology

Grammar hint

Remember that **y** is a pronoun which replaces **à** + a word in French. It can mean 'there' or 'to it/this' and it comes before the verb.

Hint

You will find most numbers in figures, but one here is written in words.

1   Read the article below.

> Nous avons demandé aux ados: << Pourquoi est-ce que vous utilisez Internet? >> Les réponses qu'on a reçues étaient intéressantes.
>
> - 95% des jeunes utilisent Internet tous les jours.
> - La majorité, c'est-à-dire cinquante-neuf pour cent, utilise Internet afin de faire des jeux. Certains y sont accros.
> - 50% regardent des clips vidéo, surtout les clips comiques, en ligne.
> - 35% tchattent sur des forums.
> - 30% téléchargent des chansons.
> - 25% font des recherches scolaires en ligne, mais on dit qu'ils acceptent trop facilement ce qu'on y met comme étant la vérité.
> - Moins de 5% disent qu'ils utilisent Internet pour se faire de nouveaux amis.

Answer the following questions **in English**. You do not need to write in full sentences.

(a) What percentage of young people interviewed play games online?

.... **(1 mark)**

(b) What do 30% of young people do, according to the survey?

.... **(1 mark)**

(c) Which is the least popular reason in the survey for using the internet?

.... **(1 mark)**

(Total for Question 1 = 3 marks)

 **A nightmare holiday**

2 Read Millie's blog.

> Le jour du départ, l'aéroport de Montréal était entouré d'un brouillard épais et notre vol a été retardé, ce qui m'a vraiment énervée.
>
> J'ai trouvé le vol difficile car j'ai le mal de l'air, alors je n'ai rien mangé et le vol était tellement long!
>
> Enfin arrivés à Londres, on a eu du mal à trouver une voiture à louer car il y avait une grève. Mon père était de mauvaise humeur pendant le trajet en taxi de l'aéroport.
>
> Pour comble de malchance, nos chambres d'hôtel étaient sales, même si les repas au restaurant étaient délicieux et pas trop épicés.
>
> Je vais retourner à Londres le mois prochain avec mon équipe de tennis. J'espère que tout ira mieux!

Answer the following questions **in English**. You do not need to write in full sentences.

(a) Why was Millie's flight delayed?

.... **(1 mark)**

(b) What did she **not** do during the flight?

.... **(1 mark)**

(c) Why was her dad unable to hire a car?

.... **(1 mark)**

(d) What did the family not like at the hotel?

.... **(1 mark)**

(Total for Question 2 = 4 marks)

Revision Guide
Page 36
Holiday experiences

Hint

Remember to read though all of the questions before you start answering them, as this can help you with the overall meaning.

Revision Guide
Page 80
Being green

Hint

Some of the language used in articles can be more formal or more unusual, so get used to this by practising in class and at home.

Hint

With a longer, more complex text, try reading it through once and then reading all the questions. These may give you some hints to help you understand parts of the text on your second reading. Reading all the questions through in one go may also help you to answer the questions correctly.

 **Being green**

3   Read the magazine article.

> **Il est vraiment facile d'être plus écolo!**
>
> De nos jours, tout le monde parle de choses qui ne sont pas du tout concrètes comme le changement climatique, le réchauffement de la Terre ou l'empreinte carbone. La vérité, c'est que les gestes de toute la population menacent notre monde, mais il ne faut pas s'inquiéter car il existe toute une liste de choses qu'on peut faire afin de protéger la planète.
>
> Premièrement, un geste qui aide l'environnement mais aussi économise de l'argent, c'est réduire la consommation d'énergie. Eteignez la lumière en quittant une pièce et baissez le chauffage. Pour économiser de l'eau, essayez de toujours arroser les fleurs et les plantes du jardin avec l'eau de rinçage des légumes!
>
> Un autre problème grave c'est les déchets. Au supermarché, n'achetez pas les produits trop emballés et respectez la nature, par exemple ne jetez jamais des papiers par terre.
>
> De plus, choisissez plutôt les transports en commun au lieu de prendre la voiture et surtout, sensibilisez les jeunes en leur montrant le bon exemple, car il faut qu'à l'avenir ils fassent aussi un effort pour sauver notre planète!

Answer the questions **in English**. You do not need to write in full sentences.

(a) What benefit does the author say you could gain from saving energy?

.... **(1 mark)**

(b) What tip is given for saving water?

....
.... **(1 mark)**

(c) What should you not buy at the supermarket, according to the article?

.... **(1 mark)**

(d) What example is mentioned in relation to respecting nature?

....
.... **(1 mark)**

(e) What is the main advice given at the end of the article?

.... **(1 mark)**

(Total for Question 3 = 5 marks)

 **Future plans**

4   Read this blog by Suzanne on a Belgian website.

> Je vais bientôt finir mes études au lycée.
>
> Je vais prendre une année sabbatique. J'ai enfin pris la décision après y avoir longtemps pensé. Ce sera une expérience à la fois divertissante et enrichissante qui me donnera confiance, et aussi je deviendrai plus autonome, des aspects qui sont indispensable pour tous les êtres humains, à mon avis.
>
> Ayant fini mon année à l'étranger, peut-être en Afrique, je serai sans doute prête à recommencer mes études. J'ai des inquiétudes, c'est vrai. Par exemple, serai-je un peu isolée ou même aurai-je peur? Qui sait? Pourtant, je sais que je vais passer une année stimulante avant de travailler dur à la fac afin d'obtenir ma licence.

Put a cross ⊠ in the correct box.

Example: Suzanne's time at school…

☐	**A**	has just ended
☒	**B**	will soon end
☐	**C**	was very pleasant
☐	**D**	seemed to last forever

(i) Suzanne's decision to take a gap year was…

☐	**A**	easy to make
☐	**B**	a difficult one
☐	**C**	influenced by her friends
☐	**D**	influenced by her parents

(ii) She thinks that doing a gap year will help her…

☐	**A**	be more independent
☐	**B**	be more intelligent
☐	**C**	earn more money
☐	**D**	make new friends

(iii) She feels that after her gap year she will…

☐	**A**	find university difficult
☐	**B**	be unprepared for studying again
☐	**C**	be ready to study again
☐	**D**	have earned a lot of money

Revision Guide
Page 63
Future plans

Hint

Don't let your own concerns and experiences influence your answers.

Hint

Suzanne gives two ways she believes the gap year will help her, so don't worry that one of these answer options isn't 'become more confident' – look again at the text to see what else she says.

(iv) She worries about…

☐	**A**	being lonely
☐	**B**	making mistakes
☐	**C**	getting lost
☐	**D**	not understanding the languages spoken abroad

(v) In the future she intends…

☐	**A**	to learn how to drive
☐	**B**	to be a teacher
☐	**C**	to find a well-paid job
☐	**D**	to get a degree

(Total for Question 4 = 5 marks)

Films

Revision Guide
Page 24 Films

5 Read these views about films.

> On a cherché des opinions sur les films. Voilà quelques réponses!
>
> **Alice:** Je préfère regarder les films chez moi car c'est plus pratique. Chez soi, on évite les coups de pied dans le dos, les gens qui commentent tout haut, et les mangeurs de pop-corn bruyants. On peut y être plus à l'aise et faire ce qu'on veut. Je me passionne pour les films d'arts martiaux car j'y ai déjà trouvé quelque chose de profondément noble. Par contre, je ne supporte pas les films d'épouvante car selon moi ils sont une véritable perte de temps!
>
> **Bernard:** J'aime mieux sortir au ciné parce que le grand écran me plaît beaucoup et que j'aime bien rester silencieux en regardant un film. Dimanche, je vais aller au ciné revoir *Le dîner de cons*, même si c'est un film qui n'est pas vraiment destiné au grand écran, vu qu'il n'y a pas d'effets spéciaux et peu d'action.
>
> **Karine:** Selon moi les films romantiques sont abominables. Ce qui me plaît, c'est regarder un film où on peut s'identifier au héros ou à un espion. Hier on a vu *Chasse à l'homme* et c'était palpitant. Tous mes copains l'ont trouvé vraiment génial.
>
> **Lionel:** À mon avis, un film devrait divertir plutôt qu'informer ou enseigner. Je veux tout simplement choisir un film qui me permette de m'échapper du quotidien. Alors pas pour moi les documentaires ou les films qui cherchent à sensibiliser le public!
>
> Ce qui est certain, c'est que les films restent aussi populaires qu'auparavant chez les jeunes. Selon vos réponses, le plus important, c'est de se marrer avec des potes, le titre du film n'est pas toujours important.

Hint

Think about what the prefix re- means when added to a verb in French.

Reading skills

In the passage, look for different ways of expressing what is said in the English statements. For example, in statement (a), the word oublier (to forget) is not in the passage, so try to look for other ways in which this idea might be expressed in French.

Who says what about films?

Enter either **Alice**, **Bernard**, **Karine** or **Lionel** in the gaps below.

Example: .....Alice..... likes films which have noble intentions.

(a) .... wants to forget everyday life when watching a film. **(1 mark)**

(b) .... hates horror films. **(1 mark)**

(c) .... has recently seen an exciting film. **(1 mark)**

(d) .... is planning to see a film which he / she has already seen before. **(1 mark)**

Answer the following questions **in English**.

(e) According to the article's last paragraph, what has happened to the popularity of films amongst young people?

.... **(1 mark)**

(f) What is the most important consideration when watching a film, according to the responses of young people?

.... **(1 mark)**

(Total for Question 5 = 6 marks)

Revision Guide
Page 1 Physical
descriptions

Reading skills

You will not need to
know every word in a
passage like this one.
Make sure you look out
for words which are
glossed – meanings will
be given at the end of
the passage.

Hint

Don't spend too long
on the more difficult
questions. Time
management is very
important in an exam.
If there is time at the
end, go back and try
to find an answer again
and remember to check
your answers. If you
cannot work out or find
an answer, an educated
guess is always better
than leaving a blank.

 Le père Goriot by Honoré de Balzac

6   Read the extract from the text.
     The author is describing a young woman, Victorine.

> Victorine est entrée dans le vestibule. Elle était très mince aux
> cheveux blonds. Ses yeux gris mélangés de noir étaient à la fois
> tristes et doux. Ses vêtements peu coûteux trahissaient des formes
> jeunes. Heureuse, elle aurait été ravissante et elle aurait pu lutter
> avec les plus belles jeunes filles. Il lui manquait ce qui crée la vraie
> beauté – elle n'était ni timide ni confiante. Son père croyait avoir
> des raisons pour ne pas la reconnaître, refusait de la garder près de
> lui, ne lui accordait que six cents francs par an, et avait dénaturé sa
> fortune, car il voulait la donner en entier à son fils. Parente éloignée
> de la mère de Victorine, qui jadis* était venue mourir de désespoir
> chez elle, Madame Couture, la propriétaire de pensionnat où elle
> vivait, prenait soin de l'orpheline comme de son enfant.
>
> ***jadis** = formerly*
>
> (Adapted and abridged from *Le père Goriot* by Honoré de Balzac)

(i)   What do we learn from the text?
      Put a cross ⊠ next to each one of the **three** correct boxes.

Example	Victorine entered the hall.	✗
A	Victorine's eyes expressed conflicting emotions.	☐
B	She is described as being shy.	☐
C	Her clothes were expensive.	☐
D	She seemed happy.	☐
E	She lacked something which prevented her being considered really beautiful.	☐
F	She had a close relationship with her father.	☐
G	Her father wanted to give his son all his money.	☐

(3 marks)

Answer the following questions **in English**.

(ii) What had happened to Victorîne's mother?

.... **(1 mark)**

(iii) What role had Madame Couture taken in Victorine's life?

.... **(1 mark)**

(Total for Question 6 = 5 marks)

SECTION B
Questions and answers in **French**

 Être en forme en janvier

7   Lis le blog de Polly.

Revision Guide
Page 13
Food and drink

> Il vaudrait mieux ne pas boire d'alcool car c'est une drogue et il est
> très facile d'y devenir accro. Après avoir célébré Noël, on devrait se
> désintoxiquer. Il faudrait aussi qu'on retourne à la salle de sport afin de
> retrouver la forme, mais faites attention à ne pas faire trop d'exercice
> au début.
>
> Pourquoi ne pas suivre un régime? Consommez moins de sucreries et
> plus de nourriture bio, comme les légumes de saison. Comme ça on
> perdra du poids et on se sentira mieux.
>
> Ma sœur cadette, Daisy, est toujours vraiment mince, mais elle est
> accro au chocolat et elle en mange beaucoup tous les jours. Malgré ça
> elle ne prend jamais de poids. Quant à moi, si je ne fais pas attention à
> ce que je mange, je grossis facilement. Ce n'est pas juste car je mange
> du chocolat uniquement le week-end.

Hint

Look for precise details
in the text as some
of the answer options
might be partially
correct.

Grammar hint

You will sometimes see
the conditional tense
in reading passages.
It is used to translate
the English 'would do
something'. You might
know it best in je
voudrais or j'aimerais
(I would like).

To form it you use
the stem of the
future tense but add
the endings of the
imperfect tense.

Mets une croix ⊠ dans la case correcte.

Exemple: Selon Polly, l'alcool…

☐	**A**	est bon pour la santé
☐	**B**	est facile à acheter
✗	**C**	est comme une drogue
☐	**D**	ne présente pas de problèmes

(i) Polly dit qu'en janvier il vaut mieux…

☐	**A**	éviter les drogues
☐	**B**	éviter le vin et la bière
☐	**C**	éviter le tabac
☐	**D**	sortir trop le week-end

(ii) Elle dit que pour commencer, il faut…

☐	**A**	faire beaucoup d'exercice physique
☐	**B**	faire de la musculation tous les jours
☐	**C**	commencer à faire un peu d'exercice
☐	**D**	renoncer au sport

Vocab hint

Make sure you know
your negative forms.
They completely
change the sense of
the sentence.

ne...pas not

ne...jamais never

ne...aucun not one

ne...ni...ni neither...nor

(iii) Selon elle, on doit…

	A	prendre du poids
	B	manger plus de sucre
	C	consommer plus de légumes
	D	éviter les légumes

(iv) Daisy…

	A	ne mange jamais de chocolat
	B	prend beaucoup de poids
	C	est assez grosse
	D	mange du chocolat chaque jour

(v) Polly…

	A	pense que Daisy a de la chance
	B	ne mange jamais de chocolat
	C	ne fait jamais attention à ce qu'elle mange
	D	est fille unique

(Total for Question 7 = 5 marks)

 **Les gîtes**

 Revision Guide
Page 36 Holiday experiences

8 Lis ces commentaires sur un site Internet.

La Corse:	Nous avons passé un séjour délicieux en Corse grâce au gîte exceptionnel qui était entouré d'arbres fruitiers de toutes sortes. Nous nous sentions comme chez nous et nous avons pu profiter du calme. Malheureusement le garage était fermé à clef.
La Bretagne:	Notre gîte n'avait pas assez d'équipements et nous étions déçus par l'absence de four à micro-ondes. Heureusement qu'on avait trouvé une piscine chauffée dans la région.
La Normandie:	Le gîte est mal insonorisé, donc il y avait trop de bruit venant de la route juste derrière le gîte. On est obligé de tout fermer si on veut bien dormir. La salle de bains est vraiment trop petite (minuscule lavabo, pas de tablette pour poser des produits de toilette).
La Provence:	Accueil chaleureux, rien à améliorer, tout est parfait. Nous y reviendrons et conseillerons cette étape autour de nous. Nous aimerions toujours trouver autant de gentillesse dans les gîtes. Encore merci!

Reading skills

Look carefully for synonyms or words which can lead you to the correct answer. For example, **cuisine** (question (a)) is not mentioned in the text. Similarly for question (b), look for words related to **circulation**.

C'est quel gîte? Choisis entre: **Corse**, **Bretagne**, **Normandie** et **Provence**.

Chacun des mots peut être utilisé plusieurs fois.

Exemple: L'accueil était super en ....Provence.......

(a) La cuisine était mal équipée en .... **(1 mark)**

(b) Il y avait de la circulation tout près en .... **(1 mark)**

(c) Il y avait plein d'arbres en .... **(1 mark)**

(d) On va revenir au gîte en .... **(1 mark)**

(e) On ne pouvait pas se laver facilement en ....
(1 mark)

(Total for Question 8 = 5 marks)

Revision Guide
Page 57
Problems and
pressures

Hint

It is fine to use words
and phrases from the
passage but do so
with caution. Try not
to copy chunks from
the passage as this
might not answer
the specific question
correctly. Look for ways
of expressing the ideas
in the passage in your
own words to suit your
answer.

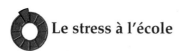 **Le stress à l'école**

9 Lis cet article d'un magazine belge.

Le contrôle du stress

Il faut d'abord savoir que nous vivons tous un stress généré par nos conditions de vie. Il existe donc en nous, au départ, un certain niveau de stress qui contribue à améliorer notre rendement. Au-delà de ce niveau, la qualité de notre performance commence à baisser et le stress de l'examen ne fait que s'ajouter au stress déjà existant.

En d'autres termes, selon ce qui vous arrive dans la vie, vous vous présentez à un examen avec un niveau de stress initial déjà plus ou moins élevé. Plus celui-ci est élevé, plus il sera facile de dépasser le niveau critique de stress. Si on ne fait pas d'effort pour diminuer le stress, on risque de ressentir une vraie panique!

Il n'y a pas de mauvaises méthodes pour se détendre. Avant un examen, on devrait avoir assez de sommeil la veille et on pourrait faire de l'exercice physique ou même passer quelques bons moments en famille.

Il peut être efficace de prendre quelques minutes pendant un examen pour vous rappeler un moment agréable que vous avez vécu, un moment de détente où vous vous sentiez particulièrement bien. Commencez par retrouver les images de ce souvenir au moment précis où vous vous sentiez bien; en d'autres termes, revoyez l'endroit où vous étiez. Puis, pensez aux bruits, aux sons associés à ce souvenir; enfin, retrouvez les autres sensations (détente, bien-être) que vous viviez à ce moment-là.

Réponds aux questions **en français**. Il n'est pas nécessaire d'écrire des phrases complètes.

(a) Selon l'article, qu'est-ce qui cause le stress?

.... **(1 mark)**

(b) Que faut-il faire la veille d'un examen?

.... **(1 mark)**

(c) Que pourrait-on aussi faire avant un examen pour se détendre? Donne **un** détail.

....

.... **(1 mark)**

(d) Qu'est-ce qu'on propose de faire pendant un examen?

.... **(1 mark)**

(e) Pourquoi est-ce qu'on mentionne le bruit?

.... **(1 mark)**

(Total for Question 9 = 5 marks)

 Translation

10 Translate this passage **into English**.

> Mes copains vont souvent à la patinoire dans la ville voisine. Il est embêtant de ne pas en avoir une un peu plus près de chez nous. On vient de bâtir un nouveau centre commercial au centre. Pourtant, à mon avis, il vaudrait mieux qu'on construise un centre sportif car il n'y a rien à faire ici si on est jeune.

....

....

....

....

....

....

....

....

....

....

(Total for Question 10 = 7 marks)

TOTAL FOR PAPER = 50 MARKS

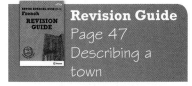
Revision Guide
Page 47
Describing a town

Translation skills

Be careful with specific items of vocabulary. Try not to leave a blank – an informed guess would be better. Here, if you did not know patinoire, you could guess that it must be a place.

Revision Guide
Page 20
Hobbies,
Page 21 Music,
Page 22 Sport

Hint

Remember that if one bullet point requires you to do two things, you must do both or you will not have covered the bullet point fully. So, in the second bullet point you need to describe what you don't like doing **and** give a reason.

Set B Writing Higher practice paper
Time: 1 hour 20 minutes

Total marks: 60
Choose either Question 1(a) or Question 1(b)

Les passe-temps

1   (a)   Dominique, ton ami(e) français(e), veut savoir comment tu passes ton temps libre.

Écris un e-mail à Dominique. Tu **dois** faire référence aux points suivants:

- tes émissions préférées à la télé
- ce que tu n'aimes pas faire et pourquoi
- une activité récente
- tes projets concernant un nouveau passe-temps.

Écris 80–90 mots environ **en français**.

....
....
....
....
....
....
....
....
....
....
....
....
....
....
....
....
....
....
....

(Total for Question 1(a) = 20 marks)

La vie de tous les jours

(b) Un site Internet suisse pour les jeunes cherche ton opinion sur la vie de tous les jours.

Écris un article pour ce site Internet.

Tu **dois** faire référence aux points suivants:

- ta personnalité
- ce que tu aimes faire quand tu sors avec des amis
- un emploi que tu as eu
- tes projets d'avenir.

Écris 80–90 mots environ **en français**.

....

....

....

....

....

....

....

....

....

....

....

....

....

....

....

....

....

....

....

....

....

....

....

....

(Total for Question 1(b) = 20 marks)

Revision Guide
Page 11 Everyday life, Page 16 Social media, Page 20 Hobbies, Page 21 Music, Page 22 Sport

Writing skills

Try to use some more complex grammatical constructions such as the perfect infinitive (après avoir / être + past participle).

Vocab hint

It is always worth learning vocabulary on a set topic, just in case it appears in the writing questions.

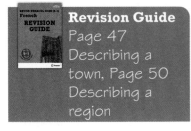

Revision Guide
Page 47
Describing a
town, Page 50
Describing a
region

Hint

It is often useful to
use connectives to link
your ideas and make
longer, more complex
sentences. In the
sample answer car, qui,
et, mais, parce que
and si are used.

Choose either Question 2(a) or Question 2(b)

Ma région

2 (a) Vous participez à une compétition organisée par le maire
     d'une ville en France.

     Écrivez un article sur votre région pour intéresser le maire.

     Vous **devez** faire référence aux points suivants:

     • une description de votre ville/village

     • votre opinion sur la région et pourquoi vous avez cette opinion

     • une visite récente en ville

     • l'importance du tourisme à l'avenir.

     Justifiez vos idées et vos opinions.

     Écrivez 130–150 mots environ **en français**.

     ....

     ....

     ....

     ....

     ....

     ....

     ....

     ....

     ....

     ....

     ....

     ....

     ....

     ....

     ....

     ....

     ....

     ....

     ....

     ....

     (Total for Question 2(a) = 28 marks)

Les vacances

(b) Un magazine belge cherche des articles sur les jeunes et comment ils passent les vacances.

Écrivez un article sur les vacances pour intéresser les lecteurs.

Vous **devez** faire référence aux points suivants:

- votre destination de vacances préférée et pourquoi
- ce que vous aimez faire en vacances
- des vacances difficiles que vous avez passées
- l'importance des vacances à l'avenir.

Justifiez vos idées et vos opinions.

Écrivez 130–150 mots environ **en français**.

....
....
....
....
....
....
....
....
....
....
....
....
....
....
....
....
....
....
....
....
....
....
....
....

(Total for Question 2(b) = 28 marks)

Revision Guide
Page 28 Holiday preferences,
Page 32 Holiday destinations,
Page 34 Holiday activities,
Page 39 Holiday problems

Writing skills

Try to use different persons of the verb as well as **je**. This will add to the range and complexity of your language.

Hint

It is good to be creative and imaginative but make sure that your answers are believable!

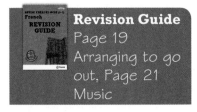

Revision Guide
Page 19
Arranging to go out, Page 21
Music

Grammar hint

Be careful to get the verb forms correct. Here you will need **I**, **we** and **he**. Look out for instances where the word order is different. For example, 'a classical music concert' will be a 'concert of music classical' in French.

Translation

3   Traduis le passage suivant **en français**:

I usually spend my free time at the seaside with my brother. Next weekend I'll go windsurfing but he will sunbathe on the beach. Last week I went to a classical music concert with my best friend. Her father took us there by car and we had a good time together.

....

....

....

....

....

....

....

....

....

....

....

....

....

....

....

....

....

....

....

....

....

....

....

....

(Total for Question 3 = 12 marks)

TOTAL FOR PAPER = 60 MARKS

The answers to the Speaking and Writing activities below are sample answers – there are many ways you could answer these questions.

Set A Listening Foundation practice paper

Time: 30 minutes and 5 minutes' reading time

Total marks: 50

SECTION A

Questions and answers in **English**

 Hobbies

1 What do these people enjoy doing?

Listen to the recording and put a cross ☒ in each one of the **three** correct boxes.

Example	going skiing	☒	
A	going cycling	☐	
B	watching TV	☐	
C	going swimming	☒	✓
D	reading	☒	✓
E	playing chess	☐	
F	going shopping	☐	
G	going wind surfing	☒	✓

(Total for Question 1 = 3 marks)

 Family relationships

2 Your exchange partner, Malaika, is talking about her family. What does she say?

Listen to the recording and complete these statements by putting a cross ☒ in the correct box for each question.

Example: Malaika thinks that her sister is…

	A	lazy
☐	B	hard-working
☐	C	funny
☒	D	chatty

(i) Malaika's brother…

☒	A	gets on Malaika's nerves	✓
☐	B	does nothing to help at home	
☐	C	is older than Malaika	
☐	D	is always well behaved	

(ii) Malaika gets on well with her mother because…

☐	A	she is generous	
☐	B	she allows Malaika a lot of freedom	
☒	C	they like the same things	✓
☐	D	she is understanding	

(iii) Malaika says that her dad…

☐	A	is very sporty	
☐	B	is quite strict	
☒	C	makes people laugh	✓
☐	D	is difficult to get on with	

(Total for Question 2 = 3 marks)

 Part-time jobs

3 Your exchange partner and her friends are talking about jobs. What do they say?

Listen to the recording and put a cross ☒ next to each one of the **three** correct statements.

		Luc	Paul	Isabelle	
Example	I work in a supermarket.	☒	☐	☐	
A	I like working outdoors.	☐	☐	☐	
B	I work on Saturdays.	☐	☐	☐	
C	I do babysitting.	☐	☐	☐	
D	I don't like my part-time job.	☐	☐	☒	✓
E	My job is well paid.	☐	☐	☐	
F	I work for a member of my family.	☐	☒	☐	✓
G	I get on with my boss.	☒	☐	☐	✓

(Total for Question 3 = 3 marks)

 Future plans

4 Your exchange partner is telling you what his friends, Alice, Dominique and Katy, want to do later in life.

Listen to the recording and put a cross ☒ in each one of the three correct boxes.

		Alice	Dominique	Katy	
Example	work in IT	☒	☐	☐	
A	travel abroad	☒	☐	☐	✓
B	get married	☐	☐	☐	
C	have children	☐	☐	☒	✓
D	become a singer	☐	☐	☐	
E	do voluntary work	☐	☒	☐	✓
F	go to university	☐	☐	☐	
G	become rich	☐	☐	☐	

(Total for Question 4 = 3 marks)

 The internet

5 You are listening to your exchange partner's mother talking about the internet. What does she tell you?

Listen to the recording and answer the following questions **in English**.

(a) What does she do from time to time?
download music ✓ (1 mark)

(b) Why does she shop online?
it's easy ✓ (1 mark)

(c) What did she do yesterday online?
researched a magazine article / did some research ✓ (1 mark)

(d) With whom is she going to speak next weekend?
a friend in Canada ✓ (1 mark)

(Total for Question 5 = 4 marks)

 Holidays

6 Sandra and Lionel are talking about holidays. What do they say they do on holiday?

Complete the sentences. Use the correct word or phrase from the box.

plays football ~~plays volleyball~~ goes sailing sunbathes
visits museums goes wind surfing buys presents visits castles

(a) Sandra plays volleyball and sunbathes ✓ (1 mark)
(b) Lionel goes sailing ✓ and buys presents ✓ (2 marks)

(Total for Question 6 = 3 marks)

 Helping others

7 During an internet link with your exchange school, Marc tells you what he does to be helpful.

What does he say that he does to help others?

Listen to the recording and put a cross ☒ in each one of the **three** correct boxes.

Example	babysits for his aunt	☒	
A	listens to his friends' problems	☐	
B	volunteers at an animal shelter	☐	
C	gives money to the homeless	☒	✓
D	does shopping for an old lady	☒	✓
E	gives blood	☐	
F	walks the neighbour's dog	☐	
G	helps his brother with homework	☒	✓

(Total for Question 7 = 3 marks)

 Helping the environment

8 You hear this interview on Belgian radio.

Listen to the interview and answer the following questions **in English**.

(a) What does Simon do every day?
recycles newspapers ✓ (1 mark)

(b) What does he say we must do?
save petrol ✓ (1 mark)

(c) What is he going to ask his parents to do?
turn down the central heating ✓ (1 mark)

(Total for Question 8 = 3 marks)

A French town

9 Your French friend, Aline, is telling you about her town.

Listen to what she says and complete the sentences by putting a cross ☒ in the correct box for each question.

Example: Aline lives in the…

☐	A	North
☐	B	South
☐	C	East
☒	D	West

(i) Her house…

☐	A	is quite small	
☒	B	has no garden	✓
☐	C	is in the town centre	
☐	D	has three bedrooms	

(ii) In her town you cannot…

☐	A	go to the cinema	
☒	B	go ice skating	✓
☐	C	go swimming	
☐	D	visit a castle	

(iii) Yesterday she…

☒	A	went out for a meal in town	✓
☐	B	went shopping in town	
☐	C	went to church in town	
☐	D	went bowling in town	

(iv) In the future she would like to live…

☒	A	abroad	✓
☐	B	in the countryside	
☐	C	in the mountains	
☐	D	at the seaside	

(Total for Question 9 = 4 marks)

1   2   3   4   5   6

 Planning to go out

10 You hear two friends, Annie and Jamel, discussing a visit to
a concert.

Listen to the conversation and answer the following questions
in English.

(a) When is the concert taking place?
.....tomorrow..... ✓ .... **(1 mark)**

(b) How much does it cost to watch the concert?
.....it's free..... ✓ .... **(1 mark)**

(c) What kind of music does Annie not like?
.....classical..... ✓ .... **(1 mark)**

(d) What are the friends planning to do after the concert?
.....go for a walk..... ✓ .... **(1 mark)**

(Total for Question 10 = 4 marks)

 A school exchange

11 You hear your friend, Lucas, talking about a school exchange he
has been on.

What does he talk about?

Listen to the recording and put a cross ☒ in each one of the **three**
correct boxes.

Example	the journey to England	☒	
A	lunches at the English school	☒	✓
B	maths lessons	☐	
C	a visit to a theme park	☐	
D	the teachers in England	☒	✓
E	a theatrical event	☒	✓
F	a sporting event	☐	
G	homework	☐	

(Total for Question 11 = 3 marks)

7

 Role models

12 You hear this report about role models on French radio.

Listen to the report and answer the following questions **in English.**

(a) Why does Gilbert respect his grandfather?
.....always smiling..... ✓ .... **(1 mark)**

(b) Where was his grandfather brought up?
.....Switzerland..... ✓ .... **(1 mark)**

(c) What does Gilbert hope to do in the future?
.....be a doctor (like his grandfather)..... ✓ .... **(1 mark)**

(d) What quality does Gilbert admire in his favourite footballer?
.....hard-working..... ✓ .... **(1 mark)**

(Total for Question 12 = 4 marks)

8

SECTION B
Questions and answers in **French**

 La routine

13 Carole parle de sa routine.

Complète les phrases en choisissant un mot ou des mots dans la
case. Il y a des mots que tu n'utiliseras pas.

tard	en car	en voiture	théâtre	vélo	avec ses copines
~~paresseuse~~	manger	lire	faire les devoirs	tôt	judo

Exemple: Carole est .....paresseuse.....

(a) D'habitude, Carole doit se lever .....tôt..... ✓ **(1 mark)**

(b) Elle n'a pas le temps de .....manger..... ✓ le matin. **(1 mark)**

(c) Elle va à l'école .....en car..... ✓ **(1 mark)**

(d) Carole fait du .....théâtre..... ✓ une fois par semaine. **(1 mark)**

(e) Le soir, elle n'aime pas .....faire les devoirs..... ✓ **(1 mark)**

(Total for Question 13 = 5 marks)

 Les copains

14 Olivier parle de ses copains.

Comment sont ses amis? Choisis entre: **amusant, actif, bavard** et
intelligent.

Chacun des mots peut être utilisé plusieurs fois.

Exemple: Marcus est .....actif.....

(a) Yann est .....bavard..... ✓ **(1 mark)**

(b) Hélio est .....intelligent..... ✓ **(1 mark)**

(c) Olivier trouve Jules très .....amusant..... ✓ **(1 mark)**

(d) Son frère, André, est .....amusant..... ✓ **(1 mark)**

(e) Victor est .....actif..... ✓ **(1 mark)**

(Total for Question 14 = 5 marks)
TOTAL FOR PAPER = 50 MARKS

9

Set A Speaking Foundation practice paper

**Time: 19–21 minutes (total), which includes
12 minutes' preparation time**

Role play

Topic: Travel and tourist transactions

Instructions to candidates

You are talking to the receptionist at a hotel in France. The teacher will
play the role of the receptionist and will speak first.

You must address the receptionist as *vous*.
You will talk to the teacher using the five prompts below.

• where you see – ? – you must ask a question
• where you see – ! – you must respond to something you have not
prepared

Task

> *Vous parlez avec le/la réceptionniste d'un hôtel en France.*
> 1. Chambre – nombre de personnes
> 2. Étage préféré
> 3. !
> 4. Petit-déjeuner désiré
> 5. ? Parking

Prepare your answer in this space, using the prompts above.
Then play the audio file of the teacher's part and speak your
answer in the pauses. You can find a full sample answer of
another student's response in the answer section.

Sample answers and teacher script

T: Je peux vous aider?
S: Je voudrais une chambre pour deux personnes, s'il vous plaît.
T: Vous préférez quel étage?
S: Je préfère une chambre au premier étage.
T: Certainement. Où voulez-vous manger ce soir?
S: Je veux manger dans le restaurant.
T: D'accord. Que voulez-vous manger au petit-déjeuner?
S: Je veux des céréales.
T: Très bien.
S: Il y a un parking à l'hôtel?
T: Ah oui, à gauche de l'entrée.

10

Picture-based task
Topic: Holidays

Regarde la photo et prépare des réponses sur les points suivants:

• la description de la photo
• ton opinion sur les vacances au bord de la mer
• des vacances récentes
• où tu vas aller en vacances l'année prochaine
• ton opinion sur les moyens de transport pour les vacances

Prepare your answer in this space, using the prompts above.
Then play the audio file of the teacher's part and speak your
answer in the pauses. You can find a full sample answer of
another student's response in the answer section.

Teacher script and sample answers

• Décris-moi la photo.
  Sur la photo il y a beaucoup de personnes sur une plage. Des gens
  nagent dans la mer et d'autres bronzent sur le sable. Il fait chaud et
  tout le monde est content. Je crois que c'est en été, peut-être dans
  le sud de la France.
• Moi, j'aime les vacances au bord de la mer. Et toi?
  Oui, j'aime les vacances au bord de la mer parce que j'adore les
  sports nautiques, surtout la planche à voile car c'est passionnant.
• Parle-moi de tes vacances de l'année dernière.
  L'année dernière, j'ai passé mes vacances en Espagne avec mes
  parents. Nous avons logé dans un hôtel moderne et confortable à
  Barcelone et je me suis très bien amusé.
• Où vas-tu aller en vacances l'année prochaine?
  L'année prochaine, je vais aller à Biarritz dans le sud de la France.
  J'espère y faire du surf pour la première fois et j'ai l'intention
  d'acheter des souvenirs pour mes copains.
• Quel moyen de transport est-ce que tu préfères pour aller
  en vacances?
  Moi, j'aime mieux voyager en avion car c'est rapide et assez facile,
  mais je déteste voyager en car parce que je trouve ça ennuyeux.

11

Conversation

1 Parle-moi de ta famille.
2 Qu'est-ce que tu as fait le week-end dernier?
3 Quelle est ta fête préférée? Pourquoi?
4 Qu'est-ce que tu voudrais faire comme emploi à l'avenir?
5 Qu'est-ce que tes parents font comme travail?
6 Quelles sont tes qualités personnelles?

Prepare your answer in this space, using the prompts above.
Then play the audio file of the teacher's part and speak your
answer in the pauses. You can find a full sample answer of
another student's response in the answer section.

Sample answers

1 Dans ma famille il y a quatre personnes. J'ai un frère cadet
   qui m'embête tout le temps parce qu'il parle sans cesse. Je
   m'entends bien avec ma mère car elle m'écoute, mais mon
   père est trop strict.
2 Le week-end dernier, je suis allé en ville avec mes copains et
   nous avons fait les magasins ensemble. J'ai acheté un jean
   et des baskets. Dimanche soir, j'ai joué au tennis avec mon
   meilleur ami et heureusement, j'ai gagné.
3 Je préfère Noël parce que j'aime donner et recevoir des
   cadeaux. J'adore décorer la maison et tout le monde est
   heureux et généreux.
4 À l'avenir, je voudrais devenir professeur car c'est un métier
   assez bien payé et j'aimerais travailler avec les enfants.
5 Mon père est électricien et il aime bien son travail parce
   qu'il gagne beaucoup d'argent. Ma mère travaille dans un
   bureau en ville mais elle trouve son emploi frustrant.
6 On dit que je suis dynamique et travailleur mais mes parents
   pensent que je suis trop bavard. Au collège, je suis toujours
   poli et prêt à aider tout le monde.

12

Set A Reading Foundation practice paper
Time: 45 minutes

Total marks: 50

SECTION A

Questions and answers in **English**

Answer ALL questions. Write your answers in the spaces provided. Some questions must be answered with a cross in a box ⊠. If you change your mind about an answer, put a line through the box ⊠ and then mark your new answer with a cross ⊠.

 Holiday preferences

1 Read the opinions about holidays on a website.

Janine:	Je vais toujours au bord de la mer car nager, c'est ma passion. J'aime aussi me faire bronzer et faire les magasins!
Thomas:	Je n'aime pas les vacances actives. Pour moi, il est important de se détendre, en lisant ou en ne faisant rien.
Catherine:	Le camping me plaît bien parce que j'adore le plein air s'il fait beau, ou même s'il pleut.
Karine:	Je pense que rester à la maison, c'est ennuyeux, mais les vacances coûtent cher.

Who says what about their holidays? Enter either **Janine**, **Thomas**, **Catherine** or **Karine**.

You can use each person more than once.

Example: ..Janine.. likes shopping.

(a) ..Catherine.. ✓ likes camping. **(1 mark)**

(b) ..Karine.. ✓ thinks that holidays are expensive. **(1 mark)**

(c) ..Karine.. ✓ is bored at home. **(1 mark)**

(d) ..Janine.. ✓ likes the beach. **(1 mark)**

(e) ..Thomas.. ✓ likes doing nothing on holiday. **(1 mark)**

(f) ..Catherine.. ✓ doesn't mind what the weather is like on holiday. **(1 mark)**

(Total for Question 1 = 6 marks)

13

A new shopping centre

2 Read the advert below.

> **Centre commercial Étoile**
> Nous sommes à deux kilomètres de Rouen, tout près du stade.
> Il y a plus de cent boutiques, un ciné (douze écrans), un grand choix de restaurants et un hôtel 4 étoiles.
> Le centre est ouvert tous les jours de 8h à 22h sauf le dimanche quand on ferme à 17h.
> Club d'enfants vendredi et samedi, parking gratuit et salle de fitness.

Complete the gap in each sentence using a word or words from the box below. There are more words than gaps.

Saturdays	Sundays	fitness centre	car parks
twice a week	on Fridays and Sundays	~~2 kilometres~~
12 kilometres	shops	screens	stadium	restaurants

Example: The shopping centre is situated ..2 kilometres.. from Rouen.

(a) The shopping centre is near a ..stadium.. ✓ **(1 mark)**

(b) There are more than 100 ..shops.. ✓ **(1 mark)**

(c) The cinema has 12 ..screens.. ✓ **(1 mark)**

(d) The centre has different opening times on ..Sundays.. ✓ **(1 mark)**

(e) There is a children's club ..twice a week.. ✓ **(1 mark)**

(Total for Question 2 = 5 marks)

14

French food and drink

3 (a) Read this article about French food and drink.

> Selon un sondage récent, il est évident que les Français sont très traditionnels. Par exemple, plus de 80% prennent trois repas par jour. De plus, la moitié de jeunes dînent devant la télé et une personne sur dix ne mange pas de petit-déjeuner.

Answer the following questions **in English**. You do not need to write in full sentences.

(i) What do more than 80% of French people do?
..have three meals a day.. ✓ **(1 mark)**

(ii) How many young French people eat in front of the TV?
..half / 50%.. ✓ **(1 mark)**

(iii) What do 1 in 10 French people **not** do?
..have breakfast.. ✓ **(1 mark)**

(b) The article continues.

> Pourtant, tout le monde pense que les repas pris en famille sont les plus agréables. Presque 75% des Français déclarent manger un casse-croûte entre les repas tous les jours, et les casse-croûtes préférés sont les chips et les biscuits.

(i) What kind of meals are considered to be the most pleasant occasions?
..family meals.. ✓ **(1 mark)**

(ii) Apart from biscuits, which is the other favourite snack according to the survey?
..crisps.. ✓ **(1 mark)**

(Total for Question 3 = 5 marks)

15

Le Petit Nicolas by René Goscinny

4 Read the extract from the text below.

Nicolas is talking about a recent afternoon activity.

> J'ai invité des copains à venir à la maison cet après-midi pour jouer aux cow-boys. Ils sont arrivés avec toutes leurs affaires. Rufus était habillé en agent de police avec un revolver et un bâton blanc. Eudes portait le vieux chapeau boy-scout de son grand frère et Alceste était en Indien, mais il ressemblait à un gros poulet. Geoffroy, qui aime bien se déguiser et qui a un Papa très riche, était habillé complètement en cow-boy avec une chemise à carreaux, un grand chapeau et des revolvers à capsules. Moi, j'avais un masque noir. On était chouettes.

Put a cross ⊠ in the correct box.

Example: Nicolas and his friends were going to play…

⊠	A	cowboys
☐	B	football
☐	C	tennis
☐	D	computer games

(i) Rufus came as…

☐	A	a cowboy
☐	B	an American Indian
⊠	C	a policeman	✓
☐	D	a Boy Scout

(ii) Eudes had borrowed something from…

☐	A	his little brother
☐	B	his dad
⊠	C	his big brother	✓
☐	D	his best friend

(iii) Alceste looked like…

☐	A	a cowboy
⊠	B	a chicken	✓
☐	C	an old Boy Scout
☐	D	a policeman

16

(iv) Geoffroy likes…

⊠	A	dressing up	✓
☐	B	wearing masks
☐	C	his older brother
☐	D	playing games

(v) Geoffroy and Eudes both…

☐	A	have rich fathers
☐	B	wore checked shirts
☐	C	brought revolvers
⊠	D	wore hats	✓

(Total for Question 4 = 5 marks)

An international event

5 Read the advertisement below.

> Au mois de mai, le festival international de la danse a lieu à Menton. L'année dernière, le festival était à Brighton en Angleterre mais le temps était pluvieux, donc les danseurs ont porté plainte auprès des organisateurs. On espère qu'il fera plus beau dans le sud de la France. Il y aura plus de quatre-vingts groupes cette année.
>
> Pour les spectateurs il y a plein de bons hôtels dans la région, mais il y a également deux campings tout près de la ville pour ceux qui cherchent un logement moins cher.

Answer the following questions **in English**. You do not need to write in full sentences.

(a) What was the problem in Brighton?
..rainy weather.. ✓ **(1 mark)**

(b) How many dance groups will take part this year?
..more than 80.. ✓ **(1 mark)**

(c) Why might spectators prefer camping?
..less expensive / save money.. ✓ **(1 mark)**

(Total for Question 5 = 3 marks)

17

Volunteering

6 Read this blog by Philippe about helping others.

> Il y a un an, j'ai commencé à faire du travail bénévole pour une association caritative qui aide les pauvres en France. Tous les vendredis, je travaille dans un bureau où je classe des documents et réponds au téléphone. Je suis lycéen et je n'ai pas cours le vendredi, alors c'est idéal pour moi, mais à l'avenir je voudrais bien trouver un emploi comme médecin, ce qui me permettrait de faire des recherches afin de réduire les maladies graves dans les pays les plus pauvres. J'aimerais aussi visiter les pays où la vie est dure car je pourrais mieux comprendre les problèmes des habitants.

Answer the following questions **in English**. You do not need to write in full sentences.

(a) When did Philippe first start volunteering?
..a year ago.. ✓ **(1 mark)**

(b) Apart from answering the phone, what does he do in the office?
..filing / files documents.. ✓ **(1 mark)**

(c) Why does he want to become a doctor?
..to do research into reducing serious illness in the Third World.. ✓

(d) What reason does he give for visiting certain foreign countries?
..to understand better the problems of those who live there.. ✓

(1 mark)

(Total for Question 6 = 4 marks)

18

SECTION B
Questions and answers in French

 Aller au ciné

7 Lis ces descriptions sur un site Internet.

Rennes:	On passe *Inferno*, film américain en version originale, sans sous-titres. Réductions pour étudiants.
Dinard:	Au ciné Studio 2, film français, *Alibi*, séances à 17h et à 20h. Ce film va faire rire tout le monde.
Nantes:	Dessins animés pour les petits et les plus grands! Venez voir plus de vingt films à un prix très raisonnable.
Lorient:	Écran 4: nouveau film d'épouvante de Rémy Gallois. Pas pour ceux qui ont facilement peur. Écran 5: film d'espionnage canadien, *Le rendez-vous*. À ne pas manquer!

Quelle est la ville correcte? Choisis entre: **Rennes**, **Dinard**, **Nantes** et **Lorient**.

Chacun des mots peut être utilisé plusieurs fois.

Exemple: On peut regarder un film canadien à ......Lorient......

(a) Il y a un film en anglais à ....Rennes.... ✓ (1 mark)

(b) On peut regarder un film comique à ....Dinard.... ✓ (1 mark)

(c) On passe deux films à ....Lorient.... ✓ (1 mark)

(d) Il y a un film d'horreur à ....Lorient.... ✓ (1 mark)

(e) On peut voir beaucoup de films à ....Nantes.... ✓ (1 mark)

(Total for Question 7 = 5 marks)

 **Les vacances**

8 Lis le blog de Chrystelle.

> Selon moi, il faut aller en vacances chaque année car on peut se détendre et se reposer un peu après avoir travaillé dur pendant l'année scolaire. Puisque j'adore la chaleur, j'aime aller en Espagne ou en Grèce, mais mes parents préfèrent des vacances culturelles en Angleterre ou des vacances à la neige en Italie. L'idée de partir en vacances entre amis m'intéresse parce qu'on aurait plus de liberté. Je m'entends bien avec toute ma famille, mais on ne partage pas les mêmes centres d'intérêt. Je crois que, cet été, j'irai au pays de Galles avec ma meilleure copine et sa famille. Nous allons y faire du camping à la montagne parce que nous aimons tous le plein air.
>
> **Chrystelle, 16 ans**

Mets une croix ☒ dans la case correcte.

Exemple: Selon Chrystelle, il faut aller en vacances…

☒	A	tous les ans
☐	B	en octobre
☐	C	deux fois par mois
☐	D	en groupe scolaire

(i) Selon Chrystelle, en vacances on a la possibilité de…

☐	A	travailler dur
☒	B	se relaxer	✓
☐	C	visiter une école
☐	D	faire des achats

(ii) Elle aime aller en Espagne car…

☐	A	il y a beaucoup de choses à faire
☐	B	on peut y faire des activités culturelles
☒	C	il y fait chaud	✓
☐	D	on peut y faire du ski

(iii) Elle pense qu'on est plus libre…

☒	A	avec des copains	✓
☐	B	avec ses parents
☐	C	en famille
☐	D	avec sa sœur

(iv) Elle n'a pas les mêmes goûts que…

☐	A	ses amis
☒	B	sa famille	✓
☐	C	sa meilleure copine
☐	D	la famille de sa meilleure copine

(v) Cet été, elle va…

☐	A	en Grèce
☐	B	à la campagne
☐	C	chez sa meilleure copine
☒	D	faire du camping	✓

(Total for Question 8 = 5 marks)

 Une soirée agréable

9 Lis cet e-mail de Robin.

> Hier soir, j'ai eu un repas délicieux dans un petit restaurant qui se trouve tout près de chez moi. J'y suis allé avec toute ma famille afin de fêter l'anniversaire de ma sœur aînée. Malheureusement, le service était vraiment lent mais la vue sur la rivière était impressionnante. Tout le monde a choisi du poisson, la spécialité du restaurant, et j'ai surtout aimé les légumes. Mon père n'a pas pris de dessert car il est au régime! Dimanche, je vais célébrer l'anniversaire de mon meilleur copain au centre sportif car il adore nager et ses parents vont louer la piscine!

Complète chaque phrase en utilisant un mot de la case.
Attention! Il y a des mots que tu n'utiliseras pas.

mangé	la natation	du poisson	un dessert
sorti	le service	la vue	la maison
petite	âgée	le régime	l'anniversaire

Exemple: Robin est ......sorti...... hier.

(a) Le restaurant est près de ....la maison.... ✓ de Robin. **(1 mark)**

(b) La sœur de Robin est plus ....âgée.... ✓ que lui. **(1 mark)**

(c) Au restaurant, Robin a trouvé ....le service.... ✓ inacceptable. **(1 mark)**

(d) Toute la famille a mangé ....du poisson.... ✓ **(1 mark)**

(e) Le meilleur ami de Robin adore ....la natation.... ✓ **(1 mark)**

(Total for Question 9 = 5 marks)

SECTION C

 Translation

10 Translate this passage **into English**.

> J'habite près de mon collège. Ma matière préférée, c'est le dessin car je suis créatif. Je n'aime pas les maths parce que je ne m'entends pas avec mon prof. Hier j'ai joué au foot pour mon équipe scolaire. Après j'ai fait mes devoirs d'informatique, mais je les ai trouvés durs.

I live near my school. ✓ My favourite subject is art because I am creative. ✓ I don't like maths ✓ because I do not get on with my teacher. ✓ Yesterday I played football for my school team. ✓ Afterwards I did my IT homework, ✓ but I found it hard. ✓

(Total for Question 10 = 7 marks)
TOTAL FOR PAPER = 50 MARKS

Set A Writing Foundation practice paper
Time: 1 hour 10 minutes

Total marks: 60

Les échanges scolaires

1 Tu participes à un échange scolaire en France. Tu postes cette photo sur des médias sociaux pour tes amis.

Écris une description de la photo **et** exprime ton opinion sur les échanges scolaires.

Écris 20–30 mots environ **en français**.

Il y a des élèves et deux professeurs à Paris devant la Tour Eiffel.
Ils font du travail. J'aime les échanges car je peux parler français.

(Total for Question 1 = 12 marks)

Un festival de sport

2 Vous allez participer à un festival de sport en France. Vous écrivez au directeur du festival où vous allez.

Écrivez un e-mail avec les informations suivantes:

- quand vous voulez arriver au festival
- où vous allez loger
- les sports que vous aimez
- pourquoi vous voulez aller en France.

Il faut écrire en phrases complètes.

Écrivez 40–50 mots environ **en français**.

Madame/Monsieur,

Je veux arriver au festival le 9 juillet. Je vais loger dans un hôtel au centre de Lyon. J'adore tous les sports mais je préfère le foot car c'est un sport actif. Je veux aller en France parce que c'est un très beau pays.

Cordialement

(Total for Question 2 = 16 marks)

25

Choose either Question 3(a) or Question 3(b)

Ma région

3 **(a)** Dominique, ton ami(e) français(e), t'a envoyé un e-mail avec des questions sur ta région.

Écris une réponse à Dominique. Tu **dois** faire référence aux points suivants:

- ton opinion sur ta région et pourquoi
- ce que tu as fait récemment dans ta région
- ce qu'il y a pour les touristes dans ta région
- où tu voudrais habiter à l'avenir.

Écris 80–90 mots environ **en français**.

J'habite à Gloucester dans l'ouest de l'Angleterre. J'aime habiter ici parce que j'ai plein d'amis et de famille dans la région, et c'est pittoresque. Hier je suis allé en ville où j'ai regardé un bon film comique au ciné avec mes copains. Pour les touristes, il y a une belle cathédrale au centre-ville et les docks historiques tout près. À l'avenir, je voudrais habiter à Londres car c'est une grande ville animée et il y a beaucoup de choses à faire et à voir là-bas.

(Total for Question 3(a) = 20 marks)

26

Internet

(b) Un site français pour les jeunes cherche ton opinion sur Internet. Écris un article pour ce site Internet.

Tu **dois** faire référence aux points suivants:

- quand tu utilises Internet
- comment tu as utilisé Internet récemment
- les inconvénients d'Internet
- tes projets sur Internet pour l'avenir.

Écris 80–90 mots environ **en français**.

J'utilise Internet tous les jours car j'ai un portable, une tablette et un ordi. J'utilise Internet pour tchatter avec mes copains et rester en contact avec des amis qui n'habitent pas près de chez moi, mais je ne poste jamais de photos sur des réseaux sociaux. Hier j'ai téléchargé de la musique et j'ai aussi envoyé des e-mails. On peut devenir accro à Internet et il y a aussi des problèmes comme le harcèlement et le vol d'identité. L'année prochaine, je vais créer ma propre chaîne YouTube et j'espère avoir beaucoup d'abonnés.

(Total for Question 3(b) = 20 marks)

27

Les passe-temps

4 Traduis les phrases suivantes **en français**.

(a) I like football.
J'aime le foot.
(2 marks)

(b) My brother goes cycling.
Mon frère fait du cyclisme / vélo.
(2 marks)

(c) My parents often watch TV.
Mes parents regardent souvent la télé.
(2 marks)

(d) I like reading but I don't like listening to music.
J'aime lire mais je n'aime pas écouter de la musique.
(3 marks)

(e) Last weekend I went to the cinema and the film was funny.
Le week-end dernier je suis allé au cinéma et le film était amusant.
(3 marks)

(Total for Question 4 = 12 marks)
TOTAL FOR PAPER = 60 MARKS

28

Set A Listening Higher practice paper

Time: 40 minutes and 5 minutes' reading time

Total marks: 50

SECTION A
Questions and answers in French

 L'environnement

1 Aline parle de l'environnement.
Complète les phrases en choisissant un mot ou des mots dans la case. Il y a des mots que tu n'utiliseras pas.

beaucoup	énerve	du papier	électricité
le verre	eau	du carton	trop
bruit	les véhicules	~~protéger~~	recycler

Exemple: Aline veut ...*protéger*... notre planète.

(a) L'environnement est un problème qui ...*énerve* ✓... Aline.
(1 mark)

(b) Elle pense qu'il y a trop de ...*bruit* ✓... en ville.
(1 mark)

(c) Elle voudrait interdire ...*les véhicules* ✓... au centre-ville.
(1 mark)

(d) Hier elle a recyclé ...*du papier* ✓...
(1 mark)

(e) Ses parents n'économisent pas l'...*eau* ✓...
(1 mark)

(Total for Question 1 = 5 marks)

 Mes copains

2 Loïc parle de ses copains. Comment sont ses amis?
Choisis entre: **ambitieux, travailleur, patient** et **optimiste**.
Chacun des mots peut être utilisé plusieurs fois.
Exemple: Paul est ...*optimiste*...

(a) Luc est ...*travailleur* ✓...
(1 mark)

(b) Sami est ...*optimiste* ✓...
(1 mark)

(c) Jean est très ...*patient* ✓...
(1 mark)

(d) Alain est ...*ambitieux* ✓...
(1 mark)

(e) Georges est ...*ambitieux* ✓...
(1 mark)

(Total for Question 2 = 5 marks)

29

SECTION B
Questions and answers in English

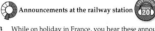 **Announcements at the railway station**

3 While on holiday in France, you hear these announcements at a French railway station.

Listen to the recording and complete the sentences by putting a cross ☒ in the correct box for each question.

Example: The next train to Bordeaux will leave from platform…

☐	A	2
☐	B	10
☒	C	12
☐	D	15

(i) The next train will…

☒	A	arrive on time	✓
☐	B	be delayed by ten minutes	
☐	C	not stop at this station	
☐	D	arrive from Toulouse	

(ii) On platform 9 there is…

☐	A	a newspaper kiosk	
☒	B	a place to store luggage	✓
☐	C	a fast train	
☐	D	a ticket office	

(iii) There is a reduction…

☐	A	for groups	
☒	B	if you buy tickets online	✓
☐	C	for students	
☐	D	for under fives	

(iv) The train at platform 10…

☐	A	will leave without delay	
☐	B	will depart at 18.00	
☐	C	has broken down	
☒	D	will be delayed	✓

(Total for Question 3 = 4 marks)

30

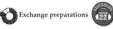 Talking about the past 🎧 21

4 Your Canadian friend, Louise, has recorded this message about herself when she was younger.

What does she talk about?

Listen to the recording and put a cross ☒ in each one of the **three** correct boxes.

Example	her hair	☒
A	the sports she used to play	☐
B	her primary school	☐
C	her character	☒ ✓
D	her sisters	☐
E	what she used to eat	☒ ✓
F	her friends	☐
G	where she lived	☒ ✓

(Total for Question 4 = 3 marks)

🎧 Exchange preparations 🎧 22

5 You overhear Louis, your French friend, talking about his preparations for a school exchange to England.

Listen to the recording and put a cross ☒ in the correct box for each question.

Example: Louis went on the exchange in order to…

	A	make new friends
☐	B	learn about English culture
☒	C	improve his English
☐	D	visit historic monuments

(i) Louis' friends…

☒	A	were worried about Louis' exchange partner's family	✓
☐	B	asked his mother to remain optimistic	
☐	C	thought he would have a good time in England	
☐	D	wished that they were going on the exchange	

31

(ii) Louis was…

☐	A	dreading the exchange
☐	B	worried about spending several weeks away
☒	C	determined not to spoil the exchange ✓
☐	D	concerned about missing his friends

(iii) His exchange partner's family were going to…

☐	A	organise visits during the day and in the evening
☐	B	try to speak to him in English to reassure him
☒	C	help him improve his language skills ✓
☐	D	take him out for a meal every evening

(Total for Question 5 = 3 marks)

🎧 A new TV game show 🎧 23

6 You hear two teenagers, Robert and Céline, discussing the latest game show on TV.

Listen to the discussion and answer the following questions **in English**.

(a) When was the game show on TV?
last night ✓ (1 mark)

(b) What did Céline especially like?
when the old lady got the last question wrong ✓ (1 mark)

(c) How do we know that the contestant on the game show was unhappy?
she was on the point of tears / crying ✓ (1 mark)

(d) Why was Robert disappointed?
the contestant won nothing ✓ (1 mark)

(e) What does Céline say about game show contestants?
they are too selfish ✓ (1 mark)

(Total for Question 6 = 5 marks)

32

🎧 Voluntary work 🎧 24

7 You overhear this conversation in a restaurant in France.
Listen to the conversation and answer the questions **in English**.

(a) Why would the boy do voluntary work?
to change his community / make a social difference ✓
.... (1 mark)

(b) For what reason would he not do voluntary work?
to gain work experience / prepare himself for the world
of work ✓ (1 mark)

(c) What would the girl hope to gain from doing voluntary work? Give **two** details.
make new friends ✓ / help disadvantaged people ✓
.... (2 marks)

(d) Give **one** reason why her friend would do voluntary work.
one of: to find herself / to gain a sense of self-worth ✓ (1 mark)

(Total for Question 7 = 5 marks)

🎧 Extreme sports 🎧 25

8 You hear a radio phone-in show about extreme sports.
Listen to the recording and put a cross ☒ in the correct box for each question.

Example: Sylvain tried bungee jumping…

☐	A	last year
☐	B	last week
☒	C	2 years ago
☐	D	2 days ago

Part (a)

(i) He wanted to try extreme sports to…

☒	A	test his limits	✓
☐	B	feel fitter	
☐	C	feel afraid	
☐	D	overcome his fear of heights	

33

(ii) He found the experience…

☐	A	awful
☐	B	really frightening
☐	C	quite good
☒	D	very exciting ✓

(iii) He thinks that lots of his friends would like to do extreme sports because…

☐	A	they might see themselves on TV
☐	B	they have read about them
☐	C	they have been influenced by his experience
☒	D	they are keen to try out what they have seen ✓

Part (b)

(i) Marianne would like to try paragliding…

☐	A	as her friends have recommended it to her
☒	B	even though it is dangerous ✓
☐	C	to overcome injury problems she has had
☐	D	because her parents say it is sensational

(ii) She thinks that she will soon be ready to…

☐	A	try ski jumping
☒	B	try sky diving ✓
☐	C	attempt a new winter sport
☐	D	become a pilot

(iii) She thinks extreme winter sports are…

☐	A	fun
☐	B	interesting
☐	C	too dangerous
☒	D	boring ✓

(Total for Question 8 = 6 marks)

34

🎧 Eating habits 🎧 26

9 You hear this interview on Belgian radio.

Listen to the interview and answer the following questions **in English**.

Part (a)

(i) Why does Mme Moulin think that Belgians are traditional?
they have / eat 3 meals a day ✓ (1 mark)

(ii) What is the presenter's reaction to her findings?
he is not surprised ✓ (1 mark)

(iii) What percentage of young Belgians do not want to eat as a family?
50% ✓ (1 mark)

(iv) What does one third of this group do only once a week?
eat at the table ✓ (1 mark)

(v) Which group of people finds eating dinner a pleasurable time?
the over 60s ✓ (1 mark)

Part (b)

(i) What does Mme Moulin often do in the morning?
skips breakfast ✓ (1 mark)

(ii) What reason does she give for doing this?
she is often in a hurry ✓ (1 mark)

(iii) What will Mme Moulin do in the future? Give **two** details.
have breakfast at least 5 times a week ✓ / not snack/eat
between meals ✓ (2 marks)

(iv) What is the interviewer's weakness?
sugary things ✓ (1 mark)

(Total for Question 9 = 10 marks)

35

🎧 An unusual festival 🎧 27

10 While on the internet, you hear an advertisement for a different kind of competition.

Put a cross ☒ in each one of the **two** correct boxes for each question.

(i) What do we learn about the competition?

Example	It is free to enter.	☒
A	It is the first round of the competition.	☐
B	The competition involves attending lectures.	☐
C	It will take place at the end of April.	☒ ✓
D	Children over 7 cannot enter.	☒ ✓
E	It is only open to teenagers who live in Rouen.	☐

(2 marks)

(ii) What else are we told about the competition?

A	The aim is to remind children that reading can be fun.	☒ ✓
B	The contestants have to write a short story.	☐
C	The contestants have to show their love of reading.	☒ ✓
D	The winners have to share their prize with the audience.	☐
E	The winners will get the chance to have a book published.	☐

(2 marks)

(Total for Question 10 = 4 marks)
TOTAL FOR PAPER = 50 MARKS

36

Set A Speaking Higher practice paper

**Time: 22–24 minutes (total), which includes
12 minutes' preparation time**

Role play

Topic: At school

Instructions to candidates

You are talking to your French exchange partner about school. The teacher will play the role of your exchange partner and will speak first.

You should address your exchange partner as *tu*.

You will talk to the teacher using the five prompts below.

• where you see – ? – you must ask a question
• where you see – ! – you must respond to something you have not prepared

Task

Tu parles avec ton ami(e) français(e) du collège et du futur.

1. Échanges – opinion
2. !
3. Rapports avec profs
4. ? Uniforme scolaire – opinion
5. ? Projets en septembre

Prepare your answer in this space, using the prompts above. Then play the audio file of the teacher's part and speak your answer in the pauses. You can find a full sample answer of another student's response in the answer section.

Sample answers and teacher script

T: Que penses-tu des échanges scolaires?
S: J'aime bien les échanges.
T: Tu as fait quelle visite scolaire l'année dernière?
S: Je suis allé à Paris avec mon école.
T: Comment trouves-tu les profs?
S: Je m'entends bien avec tous les profs car ils sont sympa.
T: C'est bien, ça.
S: Que penses-tu du fait de porter un uniforme scolaire?
T: C'est bizarre.
S: Qu'est-ce que tu vas faire en septembre?
T: Je vais continuer mes études.

37

Picture-based task

Topic: Environmental issues

Regarde la photo et prépare des réponses sur les points suivants:

• la description de la photo
• ton opinion sur le recyclage
• ce que tu as fait pour protéger l'environnement
• ta région idéale
• !

Prepare your answer in this space, using the prompts above. Then play the audio file of the teacher's part and speak your answer in the pauses. You can find a full sample answer of another student's response in the answer section.

Sample answers and teacher script

• Décris-moi la photo.
Sur la photo il y a trois personnes qui sont en train de ramasser les déchets dans un parc. Elles ont des sacs en plastique et je pense qu'elles protègent l'environnement. Elles portent un t-shirt et un jean.

• Je pense que recycler est important. Quelle est ton opinion?
Je pense qu'il est très important de recycler le verre, le papier et le métal. Sinon, notre planète sera en danger et je crois qu'il faut sauver la planète.

• Parle-moi de ce que tu as fait pour protéger l'environnement.
J'ai commencé à prendre une douche au lieu d'un bain pour économiser l'eau. Ma mère m'emmenait souvent en ville en voiture mais j'ai décidé d'aller partout en bus ou à pied.

• Comment serait ta région idéale?
Ma région idéale ne serait pas polluée et tous les habitants recycleraient tout. Il y aurait une zone piétonne en ville afin de réduire la circulation.

• Quels sont les problèmes les plus importants dans la région où tu habites?
Je pense que la pollution est un grand problème dans ma ville car il y a trop de circulation au centre-ville. Il y a aussi beaucoup de bruit, ce qui m'énerve.

38

Conversation

1 Qu'est-ce que c'est un bon ami?
2 Qu'est-ce que tu as fait récemment avec tes copains?
3 Est-ce que tu vas sortir avec ta famille ce week-end?
4 Qu'est-ce que tu aimes manger et boire? Pourquoi?
5 Comment as-tu fêté Noël l'année dernière?
6 Qu'est-ce que tu aimerais changer dans ta vie?

Prepare your answer in this space, using the prompts above. Then play the audio file of the teacher's part and speak your answer in the pauses. You can find a full sample answer of another student's response in the answer section.

Sample answers

1 Selon moi, un bon ami devrait être fidèle et loyal. Il est important de partager les centres d'intérêt et les goûts d'un ami. Mon meilleur ami est très compréhensif et il est toujours là pour moi.

2 Le week-end dernier, je suis allé au ciné avec quelques copains. On a vu un bon film comique, et après avoir quitté le ciné, on a pris un repas dans un petit restaurant qui se trouve tout près de chez moi. Le repas était vraiment délicieux.

3 Oui, je vais aller au centre sportif dimanche matin avec mon père car nous jouons souvent au badminton. L'après-midi, s'il fait beau, ma famille et moi ferons une promenade à la campagne parce que nous apprécions beaucoup la nature.

4 Mon aliment préféré, c'est les pâtes car j'adore la cuisine italienne. J'essaie de manger équilibré, mais je ne peux pas résister au chocolat. Comme boisson, j'aime l'eau minérale car c'est bon pour la peau, mais de temps en temps je prends du café le matin pour me réveiller.

5 L'année dernière, j'ai fêté Noël en famille, comme d'habitude. J'ai reçu un nouvel ordi et aussi un portable, j'ai eu de la chance. Naturellement, j'ai trop mangé et j'ai même essayé de champagne. Je me suis très amusé.

6 Je suis content de ma vie, mais je voudrais peut-être un peu d'argent supplémentaire, alors je vais chercher un petit job. Si je suis en bonne santé, je serai très heureux de continuer ma vie comme elle est.

39

Set A Reading Higher practice paper

Time: 1 hour

Total marks: 50

Answer ALL questions. Write your answers in the spaces provided. Some questions must be answered with a cross in a box ☒. If you change your mind about an answer, put a line through the box ☒ and then mark your new answer with a cross ☒.

SECTION A
Questions and answers in **English**

French schools

1 Read what Amandine has written on an online forum.

> Mon collège ne me plaît pas. Les profs nous donnent trop de devoirs. Hier, j'utilisais mon portable en classe pour chercher un mot dans le petit dico électronique et mon prof d'anglais m'a donné une retenue. J'ai dû copier des lignes et il a aussi confisqué mon portable. De plus, on n'a pas le droit de porter de bijoux, ce que je trouve bizarre. J'en ai vraiment marre.

Answer the following questions in **English**. You do not need to write in full sentences.

(a) What does Amandine say about her teachers?
they give too much homework ✓ (1 mark)

(b) Why did she get a detention?
for using her mobile / an online dictionary in class ✓ (1 mark)

(c) What does she find weird?
the rule about not being able to wear jewellery ✓ (1 mark)

(Total for Question 1 = 3 marks)

40

Music

2 Read the extract from the article about the group Daft Punk.

> Dès leur début, les Daft Punk ont fait partie des artistes français les mieux représentés à l'étranger. Les célèbres robots (car ils refusent de montrer leur identité et portent toujours des casques) ont été parmi les premiers Français de leur génération à faire danser dans les clubs mondiaux. Donc, il n'est pas étonnant de noter qu'ils ont eu des problèmes de se sentir français, surtout après avoir signé directement avec le label américain, Columbia.
>
> Grâce au succès de leur dernier album (vendu 3 millions d'exemplaires dans le monde), le duo casqué a réussi à s'implanter aussi bien aux États-Unis qu'ailleurs.
>
> À l'avenir le groupe espère faire plus de concerts dans son pays natal et ont annoncé d'annoncer deux nouvelles chansons écrites exclusivement en français.

Answer the following questions in **English**. You do not need to write in full sentences.

(a) Why are the members of the group described as robots? Give **one** detail.
one of: they refuse to show their identity (faces) / they wear helmets ✓ (1 mark)

(b) Give **one** reason why the group has had difficulty in feeling French.
one of: they signed to an American record label / group has been successful in USA/elsewhere ✓ (1 mark)

(c) What do they hope to do to increase their popularity in France? Give **two** details.
the group hopes to do more concerts in France ✓ and they have just written two songs exclusively in French ✓ (2 marks)

(Total for Question 2 = 4 marks)

41

Madame Bovary by Gustave Flaubert

3 Read the extract from the text.
Charles is a young boy who is at a boarding school.

> Charles était un garçon de tempérament modéré, qui jouait aux récréations, travaillait à l'étude, écoutant en classe, dormant bien au dortoir, mangeant bien au réfectoire. Il était fils d'un épicier qui avait été envoyé au pensionnat par sa famille.
>
> Le soir de chaque jeudi, Charles écrivait une longue lettre à sa mère, avec de l'encre rouge, puis il repassait ses cahiers ou bien lisait un vieux volume historique qu'on avait laissé à la bibliothèque de l'école. En promenade il bavardait seulement avec le domestique, qui était de la campagne comme lui.

(Adapted and abridged from *Madame Bovary* by Gustave Flaubert).

Answer the following questions in **English**. You do not need to write in full sentences.

(a) Give **two** examples of how Charles was considered to be a normal pupil.
two of: played at break / worked in study time / listened in class / slept well in the dormitory / ate in the refectory ✓ (2 marks)

(b) How do we know that he was not popular at school?
he only had one friend ✓ (1 mark)

(c) What did Charles do first, every Thursday evening?
wrote a long letter to his mother ✓ (1 mark)

(d) What did he have in common with the servant?
they both came from the country ✓ (1 mark)

(Total for Question 3 = 5 marks)

42

A shopping trip

4 Read Antoine's blog post.

> Ayant décidé de faire les magasins hier, je me suis rendu compte que, puisque j'étais tout seul, c'était une occasion d'acheter des cadeaux pour mon frère qui fêtera demain ses dix-huit ans et pour ma mère qui va célébrer son anniversaire le mois prochain. Mon père m'a emmené au centre-ville en voiture avant de partir au travail, mais j'ai cherché en vain un roman que mon frère voulait depuis longtemps. J'ai enfin réussi à lui acheter un maillot de foot de son équipe préférée à un prix très élevé!
>
> Après avoir pris un déjeuner rapide, j'ai passé une demi-heure dans une bijouterie où je cherchais sans succès une bague en argent pour ma mère. J'étais vraiment déçu, mais en rentrant chez moi à pied, j'ai remarqué une belle écharpe en soie dans la vitrine d'un petit magasin caritatif du coin. J'ai appelé ma sœur pour savoir son opinion car c'était un habit d'occasion, mais elle m'a dit de l'acheter, alors j'étais ravi d'avoir trouvé deux bons cadeaux pour ma famille!

Put a cross ☒ in the correct box.

Example: Antoine realised that he could buy presents for his family…

☐	A	because he had saved enough money
☒	B	because he was on his own
☐	C	because he was feeling generous
☐	D	because he had won some money

(i) His brother…

☐	A	has a birthday next month
☐	B	will soon be 17
☐	C	has just turned 18
☒	D	will soon be 18 ✓

(ii) His Dad took him into town…

☒	A	on his way to work ✓
☐	B	before breakfast
☐	C	because he was going shopping too
☐	D	after he had finished work

43

(iii) Antoine wanted to buy his brother…

☐	A	a football shirt
☒	B	a novel ✓
☐	C	an Italian shirt
☐	D	a football

(iv) He was disappointed because…

☒	A	he could not find a ring ✓
☐	B	he didn't have enough money for the present he wanted for his mum
☐	C	he could not find a scarf
☐	D	he did not have enough money

(v) He phoned his sister because…

☐	A	she wanted him to buy a silver bag
☐	B	he wanted to check that she had not bought the same present
☒	C	he was concerned about buying a second-hand scarf ✓
☐	D	spending money was his bad habit

(Total for Question 4 = 5 marks)

44

Future jobs

5 Read what these teenagers say about future jobs.

> Louise, 17 ans, ne sait pas du tout ce qu'elle veut faire plus tard dans la vie.
>
> Annie, 16 ans, a envie de devenir coiffeuse. Elle sait que plein de gens disent que c'est un métier qui ne sert à rien, mais elle voudrait bien rencontrer beaucoup de gens et développer des amitiés qui pourraient durer longtemps, car elle apprécie vraiment la valeur qu'on attache à l'amitié de nos jours.
>
> Les parents de René, 18 ans, veulent qu'il soit chirurgien comme son oncle. Mais lui pense qu'il n'est pas doué. Il préférerait travailler dans l'informatique mais il sait que c'est un secteur populaire, surtout chez les jeunes.
>
> Kevin, 17 ans, aimerait poursuivre une carrière qui conviendrait à ses compétences dont la créativité est la principale. Il croit qu'il sera architecte, mais il comprend qu'il faut travailler dur tout le temps et qu'il risque d'être blessé par des chutes d'objets lourds.
>
> Ellie, 19 ans, a toujours rêvé de devenir chanteuse, mais ses copines se moquent d'elle en disant qu'elle devrait être plus réaliste. Elles disent qu'elle doit penser à un emploi dans un bureau!
>
> Ce qui est certain, c'est qu'il faut choisir un emploi qu'on aime et qu'on devrait faire des recherches avant de décider ce qu'on fera dans la vie.

Who says what about future jobs?

Enter either **Annie**, **René**, **Kevin** or **Ellie** in the gaps below.

(a) __René__ ✓ does not want to follow a family career path.
(1 mark)

(b) __Annie__ ✓ would like a job which could help forge friendships.
(1 mark)

(c) __Kevin__ ✓ wants to choose a career which suits his / her skills.
(1 mark)

(d) __Ellie__ ✓ would like to follow his / her dreams. **(1 mark)**

Answer the following question **in English**.

(e) Which **two** pieces of advice are given to people about their future jobs?

choose a job you like ✓ / do research before deciding ✓

(2 marks)

(Total for Question 5 = 6 marks)

45

Homelessness

6 Read the article from a magazine.

> Sylvie Martin habite à Lyon, une grande ville où il y a plus de 8000 personnes sans domicile fixe qui vivent dans les rues de la ville. Elle vient de commencer à aider les sans-abri en travaillant pour une association caritative de la région. Le nombre de volontaires augmente lentement mais on pourrait certainement faire plus afin d'améliorer le mode de vie de ces pauvres.
>
> Elle exprime ses sentiments: «J'étais choquée par le nombre de SDF dans la ville. Il y a des jeunes et des gens plus âgés, mais ils ont tous besoin d'aide. Ils n'ont pas les moyens de se nourrir mais il est possible de les aider. On pourrait leur offrir non seulement de l'argent mais aussi leur parler car tout le monde a le droit d'être respecté.»
>
> Tous les samedis elle fait du bénévolat dans les rues où elle distribue des choses indispensables comme des sacs de couchage, des couvertures et des aliments. Mais l'association a besoin d'argent et de plus de volontaires, alors pouvez-vous faire une différence et qu'est-ce que vous allez faire afin d'aider les autres?

(i) What does this article tell us?

Put a cross ☒ next to each one of the **three** correct boxes.

Example	There are over 8000 homeless people in Lyon.	☒
A	Homelessness can affect the young.	☒ ✓
B	Sylvie has always worked for a charity.	☐
C	Sylvie was not surprised by the number of homeless people.	☐
D	She works once a week to help the homeless.	☒ ✓
E	She sometimes gives out blankets to the people in the street.	☒ ✓
F	She sometimes gives out money to the homeless.	☐
G	The charity has enough volunteers.	☐

(3 marks)

Answer the following question **in English**.

(ii) Which **two** questions is the reader asked at the end of the article?

Can you make a difference? ✓ What are you going to do to help others? ✓

(2 marks)

(Total for Question 6 = 5 marks)

46

SECTION B
Questions and answers in French

Aller à un festival

7 Lis ces descriptions sur un site touristique.

Rennes:	Le festival de la culture bretonne se passera comme toujours en avril cette année. On va célébrer la gastronomie de la région. Venez goûter tous les plats typiques!
Montpellier:	Vous aimez les sports de neige? Alors le festival de la mer n'est pas pour vous! Par contre, si vous voulez essayer un nouveau sport nautique, pourquoi ne pas venir à ce festival qui aura lieu pour la première fois en juillet?
Caen:	Pour ceux qui se passionnent pour le passé: visitez le festival de la vie au Moyen Âge en octobre. L'année dernière, on a découvert tous les secrets de la vie d'un moine à cette époque, mais cette année on verra comment vivaient les rois!
Lille:	Le festival de l'art africain aura lieu en septembre. Le dernier festival a réussi à attirer plus de cinq mille visiteurs et on espère dépasser ce chiffre cette année.

Quelle est la ville correcte? Choisis entre: **Rennes**, **Montpellier**, **Caen** et **Lille**.

Chacun des mots peut être utilisé plusieurs fois.

Exemple: Si vous appréciez l'art, allez à ……__Lille__……

(a) Un nouveau festival se passera à ……__Montpellier__ ✓ **(1 mark)**

(b) Si vous aimez bien manger, allez à ……__Rennes__ ✓ **(1 mark)**

(c) Si vous aimez l'histoire, visitez ……__Caen__ ✓ **(1 mark)**

(d) Le festival de l'année dernière à ……__Lille__ ✓…… était populaire. **(1 mark)**

(e) Si vous voulez être plus actif, allez à ……__Montpellier__ ✓ **(1 mark)**

(Total for Question 7 = 5 marks)

47

La vie à Montréal

8 Lis le blog de Paul.

> Ce qui me plaît vraiment, c'est voyager partout dans le monde afin d'élargir mes horizons. Je viens de passer mes vacances en France. De retour dans ma ville natale, Montréal, j'ai recommencé à apprécier ses charmes. Quand on croise le regard d'un passant, on sourit immédiatement et on te tutoie sans hésitation. Les touristes sont toujours les bienvenus. Dès qu'on remarque un touriste avec une carte ouverte, quelqu'un vient lui demander s'il a besoin d'aide.
>
> À Montréal, on ne court pas et on ne se bouscule jamais dans le métro, même aux heures de pointe. On célèbre la première neige avec la même ferveur que les premières températures positives – le moment où il fait plus de dix degrés, c'est l'été!
>
> Montréal n'est pas une ville parfaite. Je déteste les embouteillages interminables et je voudrais qu'on développe suffisamment les transports en commun, mais la ville, à l'image de ses habitants, est chaleureuse, reconnaissante de son histoire mais tournée vers l'avenir, ouverte, cosmopolite et délicieuse à vivre!
>
> **Paul, 23 ans**

Mets une croix ☒ dans la case correcte.

Exemple: Paul aime voyager pour…

☒	A	ouvrir de nouveaux horizons
☐	B	perfectionner ses compétences linguistiques
☐	C	se faire de nouveaux amis
☐	D	rendre visite à ses copains

(i) Paul…

☒	A	est rentré des vacances récemment ✓
☐	B	va passer ses vacances à Montréal
☐	C	est de nationalité française
☐	D	habite aux États-Unis

(ii) À Montréal…

☐	A	il n'y a pas beaucoup de touristes
☐	B	on ne se tutoie jamais
☐	C	les touristes ne se perdent pas
☒	D	on est toujours prêt à aider les touristes ✓

48

(iii) À Montréal…

	A	il fait toujours chaud	
	B	il n'y a pas de métro	
☒	C	les habitants sont plutôt polis	✓
	D	les gens sont souvent pessimistes	

(iv) Au centre de Montréal…

	A	les transports en commun sont bien développés	
☒	B	il y a beaucoup de circulation	✓
	C	la vie est parfaite	
	D	les véhicules sont interdits	

(v) Paul…

	A	préférerait vivre en France	
☒	B	aime bien vivre à Montréal	✓
	C	voudrait voyager plus	
	D	trouve les habitants de Montréal assez sympa	

(Total for Question 8 = 5 marks)

49

La guerre contre le surpoids

9 Lis cette page web.

En Guadeloupe, le surpoids est un vrai problème de santé publique vu qu'une personne sur deux est obèse, un chiffre qui est quatre fois plus élevé qu'en France. Le problème va toujours croissant, donc l'Agence régionale de santé (ARS) a déjà lancé de multiples initiatives afin de lutter contre ce fléau. Parmi elles, le programme nutrition-santé Carambole a pour but la prévention contre le surpoids en ciblant les élèves de maternelle.

En essayant de sensibiliser les très jeunes enfants, on veut établir des routines alimentaires plus saines chez une génération d'enfants pour pouvoir réduire le risque de diabète et de problèmes de cœur.

Si la majeure partie des projets de prévention et de sensibilisation concerne les jeunes, il est également nécessaire de ne pas négliger les adultes. Les femmes tout particulièrement qui, en tant que mères, peuvent être les actrices primordiales d'une alimentation saine et équilibrée.

Réponds aux questions **en français**. Il n'est pas nécessaire d'écrire des phrases complètes.

(a) Comment sait-on que l'obésité est un véritable problème en Guadeloupe?
    une personne sur deux est obèse ✓   **(1 mark)**

(b) Le programme nutrition-santé Carambole concerne qui en particulier?
    les élèves de maternelle ✓   **(1 mark)**

(c) On essaie d'améliorer la santé des jeunes enfants en réduisant quelles **deux** maladies?
    le diabète ✓ *et les maladies de cœur* ✓
    (2 marks)

(d) Pourquoi est-ce que les femmes sont particulièrement importantes?
    one of: elles sont des mères / elles sont les sources
    principales d'une alimentation saine/équilibrée ✓   **(1 mark)**

(Total for Question 9 = 5 marks)

50

SECTION C

Translation

10 Translate this passage **into English**.

Selon mes parents, je suis paresseux et ils disent que je ne fais rien à l'école. Hier soir, ils ont refusé de me laisser sortir avec mes amis car je n'avais pas fini mes devoirs. J'étais vraiment déçu. Je vais essayer d'obtenir de meilleures notes parce que je voudrais avoir plus de liberté à l'avenir.

According to my parents I'm lazy ✓ *and they say that I do*
nothing at school ✓. *Last night they refused to let me go*
out ✓ *with my friends because I had not finished my*
homework ✓. *I was really disappointed* ✓. *I'm going to try to*
get better marks ✓ *because I'd like to have more freedom in*
the future ✓.

(Total for Question 10 = 7 marks)
TOTAL FOR PAPER = 50 MARKS

51

Set A Writing Higher practice paper
Time: 1 hour 20 minutes

Total marks: 60
Choose either Question 1(a) or Question 1(b)

Ma famille

1 (a) Alex, ton ami(e) français(e), t'a envoyé un e-mail sur la vie en famille.
    Écris une réponse à Alex. Tu **dois** faire référence aux points suivants:
    • les membres de ta famille
    • tes rapports avec eux
    • une visite récente avec ta famille
    • vos projets en famille pour le week-end prochain.

    Écris 80–90 mots environ **en français**.

    Dans ma famille il y a quatre personnes: mes parents, ma
    sœur cadette, qui s'appelle Jade, et moi. Ma mère, Louise, a
    42 ans et elle est petite et belle. Mon père, Mark, est très
    grand et mince. Je m'entends bien avec mes parents car ils me
    respectent, mais, de temps en temps Jade m'énerve parce
    qu'elle est trop bavarde.
    Hier, nous sommes allés au bord de la mer où j'ai fait de la
    voile, ce qui m'a beaucoup plu. Le week-end prochain, nous
    irons en ville regarder un film comique ensemble.

    (Total for Question 1(a) = 20 marks)

52

L'environnement

    (b) Un site Internet français pour les jeunes cherche ton opinion sur l'environnement.
    Écris à ce site Internet. Tu **dois** faire référence aux points suivants:
    • le problème environnemental le plus grave selon toi
    • ton opinion sur les problèmes environnementaux
    • ce que tu as fait récemment pour protéger l'environnement
    • tes actions environnementales à l'avenir.

    Écris 80–90 mots environ **en français**.

    À mon avis, le problème le plus grave c'est la pollution. Je
    suis triste quand je vois des déchets dans la rue ou dans
    les rivières car on est en train de détruire la planète.
    Le week-end dernier, j'ai recyclé des journaux et des bouteilles
    vides au centre de recyclage et j'étais très content(e).
    J'ai aussi décidé de prendre une douche au lieu d'un bain afin
    d'économiser de l'eau. À l'avenir, j'essaierai de voyager partout
    en bus ou en train car je pense qu'il y a trop de circulation
    en ville.

    (Total for Question 1(b) = 20 marks)

53

Choose either question 2(a) or 2(b)

Une visite scolaire

2 (a) Vous voulez participer à une visite scolaire dans un collège en France, mais il y a très peu de places disponibles.
    Écrivez une lettre pour convaincre le principal de vous offrir une place.
    Vous **devez** faire référence aux points suivants:
    • pourquoi vous voulez participer
    • une visite scolaire récente
    • comment la visite va vous aider à l'avenir
    • l'importance des langues dans le monde.

    Justifiez vos idées et vos opinions.

    Écrivez 130–150 mots environ **en français**.

    Madame/Monsieur,

    Je vous écris parce que je voudrais bien participer à la visite
    que vous organisez dans votre école en France. Puisque je
    m'intéresse énormément aux langues, j'aimerais bien améliorer
    mon français et perfectionner mon accent.
    Il y a quelques mois, on a organisé une visite à Londres pour
    notre classe d'histoire et j'ai décidé d'y participer. C'était
    extra puisqu'on a visité tous les sites historiques comme la Tour
    de Londres et le palais de Buckingham. Avant de rentrer, j'ai
    même eu le temps de faire les magasins au centre-ville où j'ai
    réussi à trouver des cadeaux pour mes copains. J'aimerais bien
    y retourner!
    Selon moi, la visite me donnerait plus confiance en moi et
    j'aurais l'occasion de retrouver plein de jeunes de pays
    différents, ce qui serait génial.
    À mon avis, parler plusieurs langues est vraiment important car
    il faut élargir ses horizons et découvrir la culture des autres.

    Cordialement

    (Total for Question 2(a) = 28 marks)

54

123

Everyday life

(b) Un magazine français cherche des articles sur la vie des ados pour son site Internet.

Écrivez un article sur votre vie d'adolescent.

Vous **devez** faire référence aux points suivants:

- vos passe-temps préférés et pourquoi vous avez ces passe-temps
- un événement récent mémorable de votre vie
- un nouveau passe-temps que vous aimeriez essayer
- l'importance du temps libre.

Justifiez vos idées et vos opinions.

Écrivez 130–150 mots environ **en français**.

Je passe plein de temps à faire du sport car je pense qu'il est vraiment important d'être en forme. Je fais de l'équitation depuis plus de dix ans et j'ai mon propre cheval, que j'adore. Je vais souvent au centre sportif en ville où je pratique une gamme de sports.

Je viens de fêter mes seize ans et c'était fantastique. Mes parents ont organisé une fête chez nous et tous mes copains sont venus. On m'a donné beaucoup de cadeaux, mais ce que j'ai surtout aimé c'était l'ambiance. Naturellement, j'étais épuisé le lendemain mais c'était une journée que je n'oublierai jamais.

À l'avenir, j'aimerais essayer la planche à voile car j'adore les sports nautiques et je voudrais bien garder la forme.

Selon moi, on devrait avoir assez de temps libre car on travaille dur pendant une grande partie de l'année, et faire du sport, par exemple, est un moyen super d'oublier les ennuis de tous les jours.

(Total for Question 2(b) = 28 marks)

55

Translation

3 Traduis le passage suivant **en français**:

> I usually spend my holidays in Scotland with my family. Last year I stayed in an enormous hotel by the sea. Every afternoon my parents went shopping while I relaxed on the beach. Next summer I would like to visit Italy with my friends; I will have to earn some money, so I intend to get a part-time job.

D'habitude je passe mes vacances en Écosse avec ma famille. L'année dernière, j'ai logé dans un hôtel énorme au bord de la mer. Tous les après-midis, mes parents faisaient les magasins pendant que je me détendais sur la plage. L'été prochain je voudrais visiter l'Italie avec mes amis. Je devrai gagner de l'argent, alors j'ai l'intention de trouver un petit boulot.

(Total for Question 3 = 12 marks)

TOTAL FOR PAPER = 60 MARKS

56

Set B Listening Foundation practice paper

Time: 30 minutes and 5 minutes' reading time

Total marks: 50

SECTION A

Questions and answers in **English**

 At the tourist office

1 What do these people want to do?

Listen to the recording and put a cross ☒ in each one of the **three** correct boxes.

Example	visit the swimming pool	☒
A	visit the church	☒ ✓
B	go cycling	☐
C	go shopping	☐
D	visit a theme park	☐
E	visit the museum	☐
F	find a campsite	☒ ✓
G	watch a film	☒ ✓

(Total for Question 1 = 3 marks)

57

Where I live

2 Your exchange partner, Hannah, is talking about where she lives. What does she say?

Listen to the recording and complete these statements by putting a cross ☒ in the correct box for each question.

Example: Hannah lives…

☒	A	in the countryside
☐	B	in the town centre
☐	C	in the mountains
☐	D	at the seaside

(i) She lives…

☐	A	in quite a small house	
☒	B	on a farm	✓
☐	C	in a large flat	
☐	D	in a large house	

(ii) She doesn't like where she lives because…

☐	A	there is a lot of traffic	
☐	B	she has no friends	
☒	C	there is nothing to do	✓
☐	D	the weather is bad	

(iii) Where she lives…

☐	A	there is a shopping centre	
☐	B	there is a supermarket	
☐	C	there are no shops	
☒	D	there are two shops	✓

(Total for Question 2 = 3 marks)

58

A French school

3 Your exchange partner and her friends are talking about school. What do they say?

Listen to the recording and put a cross ☒ next to each one of the **three** correct statements.

		Sophie	Jamel	Rashida	
Example	I hate maths	☒	☐	☐	
A	I want to use my mobile in class	☐	☐	☐	
B	School is boring	☐	☐	☐	
C	School is well equipped	☐	☒	☐	✓
D	I get too much homework	☒	☐	☐	✓
E	I play for a school team	☐	☐	☐	
F	I want to wear jewellery	☐	☐	☒	✓
G	I don't like the canteen	☐	☐	☐	

(Total for Question 3 = 3 marks)

 Part-time jobs

4 Your exchange partner is telling you which part-time jobs his friends **Alice**, **Olivier** and **Chloé** have.

Listen to the recording and put a cross ☒ in each one of the **three** correct boxes.

		Alice	Olivier	Chloé	
Example	works in a supermarket	☒	☐	☐	
A	wants a different job	☐	☒	☐	✓
B	likes colleagues	☒	☐	☐	✓
C	job is badly paid	☐	☐	☐	
D	job is boring	☐	☐	☐	
E	works every evening	☐	☐	☐	
F	job is interesting	☐	☐	☒	✓
G	works in a café	☐	☐	☐	

(Total for Question 4 = 3 marks)

59

 Ambitions

5 Your French friend is telling you about her ambitions for the future.

Listen to the recording and answer the questions **in English**.

(a) What does she plan to do when she leaves school?
  go to university ✓ **(1 mark)**

(b) Where does she plan to travel in the future?
  Africa ✓ **(1 mark)**

(c) What type of job would she like?
  a job in IT ✓ **(1 mark)**

(d) What does she say about future relationships?
  does not want to get married ✓ **(1 mark)**

(Total for Question 5 = 4 marks)

 Eating habits

6 Sylvie and Louis are talking about what they like to eat. What do they like?

Complete the sentences. Use the correct word from the box.

~~strawberries~~	sweets	fruit	chips
crisps	meat	fish	chocolate

(a) Sylvie likes eating ...*strawberries*... and ...*fish*... ✓ **(1 mark)**
(b) Louis likes eating ...*sweets*... ✓ and ...*chocolate*... ✓ **(2 marks)**

(Total for Question 6 = 3 marks)

60

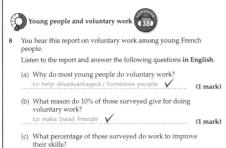

Free-time activities 🎧 TRACK 37

7 During an internet link with your exchange school, Karine tells you what she does in her free time.

What does she say she does?

Listen to the recording and put a cross ☒ in each one of the **three** correct boxes.

Example	plays table tennis	☒	
A	goes cycling	☒	✓
B	plays chess	☐	
C	reads novels	☒	✓
D	plays volleyball	☐	
E	collects stamps	☐	
F	goes water skiing	☒	✓
G	goes skiing	☐	

(Total for Question 7 = 3 marks)

Young people and voluntary work 🎧 TRACK 38

8 You hear this report on voluntary work among young French people.

Listen to the report and answer the following questions **in English**.

(a) Why do most young people do voluntary work?
to help disadvantaged / homeless people ✓ (1 mark)

(b) What reason do 10% of those surveyed give for doing voluntary work?
to make (new) friends ✓ (1 mark)

(c) What percentage of those surveyed do work to improve their skills?
12% ✓ (1 mark)

(Total for Question 8 = 3 marks)

Technology 🎧 TRACK 39

9 You hear this radio programme about internet technology.

Listen to the recording and complete the sentences by putting a cross ☒ in the correct box for each question.

Example: Jules goes on social media…

	A	very rarely
☐	B	once a week
☒	C	every day
☐	D	every weekend

(i) Yesterday Jules…

☐	A	bought a new mobile
☐	B	downloaded music online
☐	C	saw a photo of his family online
☒	D	lost his mobile	✓

(ii) He uses his computer mostly to…

☒	A	send emails	✓
☐	B	research school projects
☐	C	check sports results
☐	D	go on forums

(iii) Jules never…

☐	A	posts photos on sites
☐	B	uses his real name online
☒	C	tells anyone his password	✓
☐	D	lets other people use his computer

(iv) Tomorrow he is going to…

☐	A	change his password
☐	B	buy a new tablet
☒	C	ask his parents for help	✓
☐	D	contact friends in Scotland

(Total for Question 9 = 4 marks)

Primary school 🎧 TRACK 40

10 Your French friend, Lucille, is telling you about her old primary school.

Listen to what she says and answer the questions **in English**.

(a) What did she like best about her primary school?
food / lunches ✓ (1 mark)

(b) What did she do at break on most days?
chatted to friends ✓ (1 mark)

(c) What does she say about her teachers?
respected them ✓ (1 mark)

(d) What rule did she used to hate?
not being allowed to eat in class ✓ (1 mark)

(Total for Question 10 = 4 marks)

Issues in town 🎧 TRACK 41

11 Your Belgian friend, Marouane, has recorded this message about helping the environment in his home town.

What does he talk about?

Listen to the recording and put a cross ☒ in each one of the **three** correct boxes.

Example	installing more litter bins	☒	
A	creating traffic-free zones	☒	✓
B	saving electricity	☐	
C	improving public transport	☒	✓
D	reducing noise pollution	☒	✓
E	improving the quality of graffiti	☐	
F	creating green belts	☐	
G	installing solar panels	☐	

(Total for Question 11 = 3 marks)

A difficult holiday 🎧 TRACK 42

12 You hear this interview on French radio about a disastrous holiday.

Listen to the interview and answer the following questions **in English**.

(a) How did Salika find the flight to Morocco?
pleasant ✓ (1 mark)

(b) What was the problem with the hotel's location? Give **one** detail.
one of: it was 10 km from the coast / not on the coast / not as stated in the brochure ✓ (1 mark)

(c) What does Salika say about the food in the hotel?
too spicy ✓ (1 mark)

(d) How is the hotel owner described?
rude / impolite ✓ (1 mark)

(Total for Question 12 = 4 marks)

SECTION B
Questions and answers in **French**

Les rapports 🎧 TRACK 43

13 Gabriel parle de sa famille.

Complète les phrases en choisissant un mot ou des mots dans la case. Il y a des mots que tu n'utiliseras pas.

son frère aîné	~~sa sœur cadette~~	drôle	énervant
stricte	compréhensive	son petit frère	l'équitation
le cyclisme	parfois	rarement	

Exemple: Louise est _sa sœur cadette_

(a) Gabriel s'entend mieux avec _son frère aîné_ ✓ (1 mark)

(b) Il trouve Robert _énervant_ ✓ (1 mark)

(c) Il dit que sa mère est très _stricte_ ✓ (1 mark)

(d) Son père aime _l'équitation_ ✓ (1 mark)

(e) Gabriel fait de la natation _parfois_ ✓ (1 mark)

(Total for Question 13 = 5 marks)

Mes collègues 🎧 TRACK 44

14 Yolande parle de son travail.

Comment sont ses collègues? Choisis entre: **amusante**, **agaçante**, **gentille** et **généreuse**.

Chacun des mots peut être utilisé plusieurs fois.

Exemple: Nancy est _gentille_

(a) Pauline est très _amusante_ ✓ (1 mark)

(b) Monique n'est pas _amusante_ ✓ (1 mark)

(c) Olivia est toujours _généreuse_ ✓ (1 mark)

(d) Connie est vraiment _agaçante_ ✓ (1 mark)

(e) Julie est _gentille_ ✓ (1 mark)

(Total for Question 14 = 5 marks)
TOTAL FOR PAPER = 50 MARKS

Set B Speaking Foundation practice paper

Time: 19–21 minutes (total), which includes 12 minutes' preparation time

Role play

Topic: Friends and families 🎧 TRACK 45

Instructions to candidates

You are talking about your family and friends with your French friend. The teacher will play the role of your friend and will speak first.

You must address your French friend as *tu*.

You will talk to the teacher using the five prompts below.

• where you see – ? – you must ask a question
• where you see – ! – you must respond to something you have not prepared

Task

Tu parles de la famille et des amis avec ton ami(e) français(e).
1. Membre de ta famille – description
2. Ta famille – **ton** opinion
3. !
4. Activité préférée avec ta famille
5. ? Meilleur copain

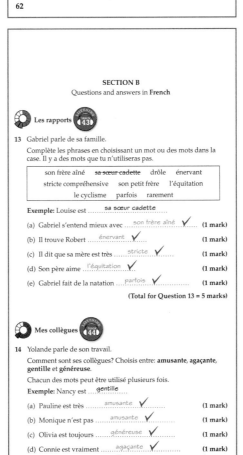

Prepare your answer in this space, using the prompts above. Then play the audio file of the teacher's part and speak your answer in the pauses. You can find a full sample answer of another student's response in the answer section.

Sample answers and teacher script 🎧 TRACK 45

T: Décris-moi quelqu'un de ta famille.
P: Ma sœur est assez grande et mince.
T: Que penses-tu de ta famille?
P: J'adore ma famille.
T: Tu préfères sortir avec tes amis ou avec ta famille?
P: Je préfère sortir avec mes amis car c'est plus amusant.
T: Quelle est ton activité préférée avec ta famille?
P: Je préfère aller au ciné avec ma famille car c'est intéressant.
T: Ah bon!
P: Tu as un meilleur copain?
T: Non, mais j'ai plein d'amis.

Picture-based task

Topic: Future studies

Regarde la photo et prépare des réponses sur les points suivants:

- la description de la photo
- ton opinion sur les avantages d'aller à l'université
- les matières que tu as trouvées utiles au collège
- tes projets pour septembre prochain
- ton opinion sur les apprentissages

Prepare your answer in this space, using the prompts above. Then play the audio file of the teacher's part and speak your answer in the pauses. You can find a full sample answer of another student's response in the answer section.

Sample answers and teacher script

- *Décris-moi la photo.*

  Il y a un groupe d'étudiants à l'université. Les étudiants ont un diplôme et tout le monde est content. Les étudiants sourient et la fille qui porte des lunettes est très heureuse. À mon avis, c'est en été mais il y a des nuages dans le ciel.

- *Je pense qu'aller à l'université est une bonne idée. Et toi?*

  Je pense que c'est une bonne idée parce qu'on peut trouver un emploi mieux payé.

- *Tu as trouvé quelles matières utiles au collège?*

  J'ai trouvé l'anglais utile et aussi les maths, mais je ne les aime pas beaucoup.

- *Qu'est-ce que tu vas faire en septembre prochain?*

  Je vais rester à l'école préparer mon bac. Je vais étudier le dessin, la biologie et l'histoire.

- *Que penses-tu des apprentissages?*

  À mon avis, c'est une bonne idée si on veut trouver un emploi technique.

67

Conversation

1 Tu aimes ton école? Pourquoi/pourquoi pas?
2 Qu'est-ce que tu as fait pour profiter de ta scolarité?
3 Que penses-tu des échanges scolaires?
4 Où passes-tu tes vacances normalement?
5 Où aimerais-tu passer tes vacances idéales?
6 C'est quoi, ton moyen de transport préféré? Pourquoi?

Prepare your answer in this space, using the prompts above. Then play the audio file of the teacher's part and speak your answer in the pauses. You can find a full sample answer of another student's response in the answer section.

Sample answers

1 J'aime mon école parce que j'ai beaucoup de copains ici, et je m'entends bien avec mes profs. C'est un bon collège bien équipé, à mon avis.

2 J'ai participé au club de théâtre et c'était amusant. J'ai aussi travaillé dur pendant cinq ans. J'espère avoir de bons résultats.

3 Je pense que les échanges scolaires sont formidables. Il y a deux ans, je suis allé en France avec mon collège et je me suis très bien amusé. J'ai aussi amélioré mon français.

4 Normalement je vais en Espagne avec ma famille. Nous logeons dans un hôtel au bord de la mer et je fais des sports nautiques, mais l'année dernière nous sommes allés en France et c'était génial.

5 Je voudrais passer mes vacances à New York car, selon moi, c'est une grande ville animée et j'aimerais y faire du shopping. J'aimerais aussi visiter tous les monuments célèbres.

6 Je préfère voyager en train parce que c'est assez rapide, et on peut écouter de la musique ou lire un livre pendant le trajet. J'ai peur des avions.

68

Set B Reading Foundation practice paper
Time: 45 minutes

Total marks: 50

SECTION A
Questions and answers in **English**

Answer ALL questions. Write your answers in the spaces provided. Some questions must be answered with a cross in a box ⊠. If you change your mind about an answer, put a line through the box ⊠ and then mark your new answer with a cross ⊠.

Free-time activities

1 Read these opinions about hobbies on a website.

Jacques:	Je suis très sportif, alors je vais souvent au centre sportif où je joue au volley et au basket. Je préfère les sports d'équipe.
Tammy:	Je déteste le sport. Je préfère faire les magasins ou écouter de la musique chez moi avec mes copines.
Johan:	Ma passion c'est la lecture. Je lis chaque jour mais j'aime aussi regarder la télé. Je préfère la télé-réalité.
Kathy:	Je n'ai pas beaucoup de temps libre parce que j'ai trop de travail scolaire. De temps en temps je vais au ciné.

Who says what about their free-time activities? Enter either **Jacques**, **Tammy**, **Johan** or **Kathy**.

You can use each person more than once.

Example: ....Jacques.... plays volleyball.

(a) ....Johan.... ✓ likes reading. **(1 mark)**

(b) ....Kathy.... ✓ has little free time. **(1 mark)**

(c) ....Kathy.... ✓ sometimes watches a film. **(1 mark)**

(d) ....Johan.... ✓ likes reality TV shows. **(1 mark)**

(e) ....Tammy.... ✓ likes shopping. **(1 mark)**

(f) ....Jacques.... ✓ prefers team sports. **(1 mark)**

(Total for Question 1 = 6 marks)

69

Helping the environment

2 Read the advert below about the ways in which Marco the Mole helps the environment.

Je m'appelle Marco et j'aime protéger la planète. Je prends toujours une douche au lieu d'un bain. Je recycle les journaux tous les jours et je recycle les bouteilles le lundi et le vendredi. Je prends le bus ou, pour les trajets courts, je me déplace à vélo. Quand je vais au supermarché, j'achète des produits bio. J'économise aussi l'électricité.

Complete the gap in each sentence using a word or words from the box below. There are more words than gaps.

bath	shower	glass	home	bus	green
~~planet~~	energy	paper	money	bike	cheap

Example: Marco likes protecting the ....planet........

(a) He never has a ....bath.... ✓ **(1 mark)**

(b) He recycles ....glass.... ✓ twice a week. **(1 mark)**

(c) For short journeys he travels by ....bike.... ✓ **(1 mark)**

(d) He tries to buy products which are ....green.... ✓ **(1 mark)**

(e) He also saves ....energy.... ✓ **(1 mark)**

(Total for Question 2 = 5 marks)

70

Homelessness

3 (a) Read this article about social problems.

Selon un sondage récent à Paris, il y a plus de trois mille sans-abri qui dorment dans les rues de la capitale. Naturellement ils n'ont pas d'emploi. Ils reçoivent des pièces de monnaie des passants dans la rue, mais ils ont froid, surtout en hiver, et parfois peur aussi. C'est une situation qui laisse beaucoup à désirer.

Answer the following questions **in English**. You do not need to write in full sentences.

(i) How many homeless people are there in Paris?
....more than 3000.... ✓ **(1 mark)**

(ii) Apart from a home, what else do they not have?
....a job.... ✓ **(1 mark)**

(iii) At what time of year are their problems especially bad?
....winter.... ✓ **(1 mark)**

(b) The article continues.

La plupart des sans-abri sont jeunes, ils ont moins de trente ans. Il faut encourager le gouvernement à aider ces pauvres car c'est un problème grave. Selon presque tout le monde, il y a trop de sans-abri partout en France.

(i) What does the article say about the majority of the homeless people?
....they are young / under 30.... ✓ **(1 mark)**

(ii) Who should help the homeless, according to the article?
....the government.... ✓ **(1 mark)**

(Total for Question 3 = 5 marks)

71

Le Rouge et le Noir by Stendhal

4 Read the extract (adapted) from the text below.

A family outing is being described.

C'était par un beau jour d'automne que M. de Rênal se promenait sur la plage, donnant le bras à sa femme. Tout en écoutant son mari qui parlait d'un air grave, l'oeil de madame de Rênal suivait avec inquiétude les mouvements de leurs trois petits fils. L'aîné, qui pouvait avoir onze ans, s'approchait trop souvent du parapet et essayait d'y monter. Une voix douce prononçait alors le nom d'Adolphe, et l'enfant renonçait à son projet ambitieux. Madame de Rênal paraissait une femme de trente ans, mais encore assez jolie.

(Adapted from *Le Rouge et le Noir*, Stendhal)

Put a cross ⊠ in the correct box.

Example: The outing took place in…

⊠	A	autumn
☐	B	winter
☐	C	spring
☐	D	summer

(i) The family was…

☐	A	in town	
⊠	B	at the seaside	✓
☐	C	in a house	
☐	D	in the mountains	

(ii) Mme de Rênal was…

☐	A	watching her husband	
☐	B	speaking to her husband	
⊠	C	listening to her husband	✓
☐	D	following her husband	

(iii) She seemed…

☐	A	happy	
⊠	B	worried	✓
☐	C	carefree	
☐	D	sad	

72

(left column, top)

(iv) The eldest son…

	A	was chasing Adolphe
	B	was speaking quietly
☒	C	was trying to do some climbing	✓
	D	was about 13 years old

(v) According to the passage Mme de Rênal is…

	A	about 40 years old
	B	ambitious
	C	quite happy
☒	D	quite pretty	✓

(Total for Question 4 = 5 marks)

A part-time job

5 Read what Alice says about her part-time job.

> J'ai commencé mon petit boulot dans un magasin de vêtements il y a six mois. Je sers les clients et je nettoie le magasin à la fin de la journée le samedi et le dimanche. Je m'entends assez bien avec le propriétaire et je reçois dix euros par heure. J'ai économisé un peu d'argent car je voudrais m'acheter une nouvelle robe pour l'anniversaire de ma tante.

Answer the following questions **in English**. You do not need to write in full sentences.

(a) Where does Alice work?
in a clothes shop ✓ **(1 mark)**

(b) What does she do at the end of the days when she works?
cleans the shop ✓ **(1 mark)**

(c) Why has she been saving up her money?
to buy a new dress (for her aunt's birthday) ✓ **(1 mark)**

(Total for Question 5 = 3 marks)

73

(middle column, top)

Volunteering

6 Read Delphine's blog about her favourite celebration.

> Noël me plaît bien et c'est sans doute ma fête préférée. J'adore surtout décorer le sapin de Noël et j'aime donner et recevoir des cadeaux, bien sûr. L'an dernier, je suis allé à un grand marché de Noël à Colmar et j'y ai acheté une montre en or comme cadeau pour mon petit ami.
>
> La veille de Noël, toute la famille se réunit normalement chez mon oncle où on mange un énorme repas avant d'aller à la messe de minuit. L'année prochaine tout va changer: on a décidé de passer Noël chez ma sœur aînée parce qu'elle va bientôt acheter sa propre maison.

Answer the questions **in English**. You do not need to write in full sentences.

(a) What does Delphine particularly enjoy doing at Christmas?
decorating the Christmas tree ✓ **(1 mark)**

(b) What exactly did she buy in Colmar for her boyfriend?
a gold watch ✓ **(1 mark)**

(c) What does the family usually do before church on Christmas Eve?
one of: eats (a big meal) / meets up at Delphine's uncle's house ✓ **(1 mark)**

(d) What will change next Christmas?
they will celebrate at her older sister's house ✓
(1 mark)

(Total for Question 6 = 4 marks)

74

(right column, top)

SECTION B
Questions and answers in **French**

Le tourisme

7 Lis ces descriptions sur un site Internet touristique.

Rouen:	Festival international de musique. Entrée gratuite du 11 au 14 août.
Lyon:	Festival d'art contemporain au musée Gaillard du 1er au 30 juin. Entrée 5 euros, réductions pour les groupes.
Nancy:	Festival de l'humour. Sketchs et blagues tous les soirs du 15 au 20 juillet 12 euros.
Biarritz:	Démonstrations de planche à voile du 4 au 7 septembre à partir de 11h. Location de planches 20 euros.

Quelle est la ville correcte? Choisis entre: **Rouen**, **Lyon**, **Nancy** et **Biarritz**.

Chacun des mots peut être utilisé plusieurs fois.

Exemple: On peut participer à un festival de musique à ….Rouen….

(a) On peut faire un sport nautique à ….Biarritz…. ✓ **(1 mark)**

(b) Il ne faut pas payer à ….Rouen…. ✓ **(1 mark)**

(c) On va certainement rire à ….Nancy…. ✓ **(1 mark)**

(d) On peut regarder des peintures à ….Lyon…. ✓ **(1 mark)**

(e) On peut louer un équipement à ….Biarritz…. ✓ **(1 mark)**

(Total for Question 7 = 5 marks)

75

(left column, bottom)

Les ambitions

8 Lis ces opinions sur des projets pour le futur.

Marianne:	Moi, je vais trouver un emploi comme infirmière parce que j'aimerais aider les autres. Je sais que ce n'est pas un travail bien payé, mais pour moi ce qui importe, c'est d'être heureux.
Paulette:	Après avoir fini mes études universitaires, je voudrais voyager un peu afin de découvrir d'autres pays et d'élargir mes horizons. Je ne veux pas faire comme ma mère qui s'est mariée à l'âge de dix-sept ans et qui a eu trois enfants avant d'avoir vingt-et-un ans. Je veux être plus libre.
Sylvia:	Je ne sais pas ce que je vais faire à l'avenir. Je suis trop jeune pour décider définitivement mon futur. On me dit de suivre mes rêves, mais j'en ai beaucoup!

Mets une croix ☒ dans la case correcte.

Exemple: Marianne veut devenir…

☒	A	infirmière
	B	médecin
	C	actrice
	D	informaticienne

(i) Marianne…

	A	voudrait être riche
☒	B	aimerait être contente	✓
	C	voudrait voyager
	D	aimerait un emploi bien payé

(ii) Paulette va aller…

	A	aux États-Unis
	B	en Espagne
☒	C	à l'université	✓
	D	faire du ski

76

(middle column, bottom)

(iii) Elle ne va pas…

	A	voyager beaucoup
	B	découvrir d'autres pays
☒	C	faire comme sa mère	✓
	D	goûter d'autres cultures

(iv) Elle voudrait…

	A	se marier avant l'âge de 21 ans
	B	avoir trois enfants
	C	suivre l'exemple de sa mère
☒	D	avoir plus de liberté	✓

(v) Sylvia…

	A	sait ce qu'elle va faire à l'avenir
	B	est très âgée
☒	C	a plein de rêves	✓
	D	va suivre les conseils de ses copains

(Total for Question 8 = 5 marks)

77

(right column, bottom)

Une école différente

9 Lis cet e-mail d'Amadou.

> J'habite au Sénégal et mon collège est très grand car il y a plus de deux mille élèves. On commence très tôt, à six heures et demie, et les cours finissent à quatorze heures. Je vais au collège à vélo. Dans ma classe d'anglais nous sommes quarante et tous les élèves pensent qu'apprendre au moins deux langues est vraiment important. Nous n'avons pas beaucoup d'installations mais un lycée en France nous a donné plusieurs ordinateurs et je trouve ça génial. Nous avons un terrain de sport où on fait du sport, surtout du foot. Malheureusement il n'y a pas de piscine.

Complète chaque phrase en utilisant un mot de la case. Attention! Il y a des mots que tu n'utiliseras pas.

~~Sénégal~~	de natation	français	les élèves
informatique	le rugby	de bonne heure	les sportifs
du cyclisme	tard	le foot	France

Exemple: Amadou habite au ….Sénégal….

(a) Au collège d'Amadou, les cours commencent ….de bonne heure…. ✓ **(1 mark)**

(b) ….Les élèves…. ✓ croient qu'il est important d'étudier les langues. **(1 mark)**

(c) Une école française a donné du matériel pour les cours d'….informatique…. ✓ **(1 mark)**

(d) Au collège, le sport principal est ….le foot…. ✓ **(1 mark)**

(e) Au collège, on ne peut pas faire ….de natation…. ✓ **(1 mark)**

(Total for Question 9 = 5 marks)

78

SECTION C

 Translation

10 Translate this passage **into English**.

> J'aime aller en vacances. D'habitude je vais en Angleterre avec mes parents. Nous faisons du camping parce que nous aimons le plein air. L'année dernière je suis allé au bord de la mer en Écosse. C'était formidable mais il a fait assez froid.

I like going on holiday ✓ . Usually I go to England with my parents ✓ . We go camping ✓ because we like the open air ✓ . Last year I went ✓ to the seaside in Scotland ✓ . It was great but it was quite cold ✓ .

(Total for Question 10 = 7 marks)

TOTAL FOR PAPER = 50 MARKS

79

Set B Writing Foundation practice paper
Time: 1 hour 10 minutes

Total marks: 60

Un tournoi sportif

1 Tu participes à un tournoi sportif en Belgique. Tu postes cette photo sur des médias sociaux pour tes amis.

Écris une description de la photo **et** exprime ton opinion sur le sport.

Écris 20–30 mots environ **en français**.

Il y a des filles qui jouent au basket dans un centre sportif. J'aime beaucoup le sport et je préfère jouer au tennis car c'est passionnant.

(Total for Question 1 = 12 marks)

80

Un festival de musique

2 Vous allez participer à un festival de musique en Suisse. Vous écrivez au directeur du festival où vous allez.

Écrivez un e-mail avec les informations suivantes:

• votre instrument de musique préféré
• ce que vous allez faire au festival
• la musique que vous aimez
• pourquoi vous voulez aller en Suisse.

Il faut écrire en phrases complètes.

Écrivez 40–50 mots environ **en français**.

Madame/Monsieur,

Je joue de la clarinette mais je préfère le piano. Je vais jouer au festival dans un orchestre britannique. J'aime toutes sortes de musiques, surtout la musique classique car je trouve ça très relaxant. Je veux aller en Suisse parce que je veux voir les montagnes quand j'aurai le temps libre.

Cordialement

(Total for Question 2 = 16 marks)

81

Mon école

Choose either Question 3(a) or Question 3(b)

3 (a) Dominique, ton ami(e) français(e), veut savoir comment tu trouves l'école.

Écris une réponse à Dominique. Tu **dois** faire référence aux points suivants:

• ton opinion sur ton école
• ce que tu as fait récemment au collège
• ta matière préférée et pourquoi.
• tes projets d'études pour l'avenir.

Écris 80–90 mots environ **en français**.

J'aime mon école parce que les profs sont gentils et très compréhensifs, et ils m'aident tout le temps. Il y a un bon centre sportif et beaucoup de salles de classe bien équipées. Récemment, j'ai joué au foot pour mon équipe scolaire et heureusement, nous avons gagné le match. Je préfère l'histoire car c'est fascinant et j'aime aussi les langues parce qu'elles sont utiles dans la vie. Je voudrais passer mon bac avant d'aller à l'université où j'aimerais étudier l'anglais ou peut-être la sociologie.

(Total for Question 3(a) = 20 marks)

82

Les vacances

(b) Un site français pour les jeunes cherche ton opinion sur les vacances.

Écris un article pour ce site Internet.

Tu **dois** faire référence aux points suivants:

• ce que tu aimes faire en vacances
• où tu as passé tes vacances l'année dernière
• pourquoi les vacances sont importantes ou non
• tes projets de vacances pour l'année prochaine.

Écris 80–90 mots environ **en français**.

Quand je suis en vacances, j'aime me détendre. Je me fais bronzer à côté de la piscine ou sur la plage et je lis un magazine ou un bon livre. L'année dernière je suis allé à Rome avec ma famille. Nous avons logé dans un appartement luxueux au centre-ville et j'ai tout visité. C'était fantastique et il a fait chaud! Selon moi, les vacances sont importantes car on peut oublier les problèmes de la vie quotidienne et aussi goûter la culture d'un autre pays. L'année prochaine, je vais aller au Portugal avec un groupe d'amis et j'espère m'amuser.

(Total for Question 3(b) = 20 marks)

83

Ma région

4 Traduis les phrases suivantes **en français**.

(a) I like my town.
J'aime ma ville.
(2 marks)

(b) There are lots of shops.
Il y a beaucoup de magasins.
(2 marks)

(c) The sports centre in town is new.
Le centre sportif en ville est nouveau.
(2 marks)

(d) I never like visiting museums.
Je n'aime jamais visiter les musées.
(3 marks)

(e) Yesterday I went to the castle where I bought a gift for my brother.
Hier je suis allé au château où j'ai acheté un cadeau pour mon frère.
(3 marks)

(Total for Question 4 = 12 marks)

TOTAL FOR PAPER = 60 MARKS

84

Set B Listening Higher practice paper

Time: 40 minutes and 5 minutes' reading time

Total marks: 50

SECTION A

Questions and answers in **French**

 Ma ville 🔊48

1   Florence parle de sa ville.

Complète les phrases en choisissant un mot ou des mots dans la case. Il y a des mots que tu n'utiliseras pas.

jeunes	zones piétonnes	~~un village~~	propre
une ferme	beaucoup de chose	magasins	nuls
circulation	rien	assez bons	sale

Exemple: Florence habitait dans .... un village ....

(a) Sa ville est .... sale ✓ .... **(1 mark)**

(b) Il y a quelques .... magasins ✓ .... fermés au centre-ville. **(1 mark)**

(c) Il n'y a pas ...beaucoup de chose... ✓ pour les jeunes en ville. **(1 mark)**

(d) Florence trouve les transports en commun .... nuls ✓ .... **(1 mark)**

(e) Comme problème, il y a beaucoup de .... circulation ✓ .... en ville. **(1 mark)**

(Total for Question 1 = 5 marks)

🔊 Les films 🔊49

2   André parle des films.

Que pense-t-il de chaque film? Choisis entre: **intéressant, passionnant, nul** et **marrant**.

Chacun des mots peut être utilisé plusieurs fois.

Exemple: Selon André, le documentaire était .... intéressant ....

(a) Le film de guerre était .... nul ✓ .... **(1 mark)**

(b) André a trouvé le dessin animé .... marrant ✓ .... **(1 mark)**

(c) Selon André, le film d'action était .... nul ✓ .... **(1 mark)**

(d) Il a trouvé le film d'espionnage .... passionnant ✓ .... **(1 mark)**

(e) Le film de science-fiction était .... intéressant ✓ .... **(1 mark)**

(Total for Question 2 = 5 marks)

SECTION B

Questions and answers in **English**

🔊 Christmas celebrations 🔊50

3   Your exchange partner's friends are talking about Christmas.

Listen to the recording and complete the sentences by putting a cross ☒ in the correct box for each question.

Example: Alice used to spend Christmas…

	A	with friends
	B	with her grandparents
	C	with her mum
☒	D	with her family

(i) Alice spends Christmas Eve…

	A	with her mother	
☒	B	with her father	✓
	C	with both her parents	
	D	with her friends	

(ii) She is…

	A	always happy at Christmas	
	B	fed up because she doesn't get enough presents	
☒	C	sad even though she gets lots of presents	✓
	D	really pleased as she gets lots of presents	

(iii) Yannick used to…

☒	A	look forward to Christmas	✓
	B	go to a shopping centre to buy presents	
	C	attend a church service	
	D	find Christmas too commercialised	

(iv) Yannick doesn't like…

	A	getting presents associated with technology	
☒	B	the fact that people always want the latest models of technology devices	✓
	C	not seeing his friends at Christmas	
	D	not getting the presents he wants at Christmas	

(Total for Question 3 = 4 marks)

🔊 Environmental issues 🔊51

4   Your exchange partner, Pauline, is discussing the environment with her brother.

What do they say?

Listen to the recording and put a cross ☒ in each one of the **three** correct boxes.

Example	Pauline is concerned about animals threatened with extinction	☒	
A	Pauline thinks that people are selfish	☒	✓
B	Pauline believes that lots has been done to help animals in danger		
C	Pauline's brother mentions droughts in some countries	☒	✓
D	Pauline's brother believes that flooding is the biggest environmental issue		
E	Pauline mentions islands which are under threat		
F	Pauline mentions deforestation	☒	✓
G	Pauline's brother is not concerned about rising sea levels		

(Total for Question 4 = 3 marks)

🔊 Le camping 🔊52

5   Your French friend, Annick, is describing her holiday.

Listen to the recording and put a cross ☒ in the correct box for each question.

Example: Annick likes going on holiday…

	A	once a month	
☒	B	at least twice a year	✓
	C	once a year	
	D	only in summer	

(i) She really liked…

	A	the weather	
	B	being in Britain	
	C	the outdoor pool	
☒	D	the playground	✓

(ii) She found the showers…

	A	sometimes too hot	
☒	B	always cold	✓
	C	sometimes cold	
	D	just right	

(iii) On holiday Annick likes…

	A	going camping	
	B	staying with her family	
☒	C	a bit of luxury	✓
	D	being active	

(Total for Question 5 = 3 marks)

🔊 Choosing subjects 🔊53

6   You hear your Swiss friends discussing the subjects they chose to study.

Listen to the conversation and answer these questions **in English**.

(a) Why did Julie choose English?
her friends were not doing it ✓ **(1 mark)**

(b) Why has her decision been a good one?
she has made lots of progress ✓ **(1 mark)**

(c) Why did Manon choose physics?
her teacher was understanding / explained things well ✓ **(1 mark)**

(d) Why has this turned out badly for her?
he has left / is teaching elsewhere ✓ **(1 mark)**

(e) Why was Lopez considering studying Portuguese? Give **two** details.
he had good marks ✓ his mum is from Portugal ✓ **(2 marks)**

(Total for Question 6 = 6 marks)

85

86

87

88

89

90

Set B Answers

Holides

7   You hear this interview with Marcel Dumoulin of the Quebec tourist board on the radio.

Listen to the interview and answer the following questions **in English**.

(a) What did 80% of the people surveyed say about holidays?
spend their holidays abroad with family ✓   **(1 mark)**

(b) What was the most popular holiday activity mentioned?
hiking ✓   **(1 mark)**

(c) What type of destination was the favourite, according to the survey?
sunny places / destinations ✓   **(1 mark)**

(d) Which destination has lost popularity?
USA ✓   **(1 mark)**

(Total for Question 7 = 4 marks)

Social networks

8   You hear a news programme about problems with social network sites.

Listen to the recording and put a cross ⊠ in the correct box for each question.

Example: The man usually...

☐	A	prefers to stay at home during the holidays
⊠	B	keeps his friends informed about where he is going on holiday
☐	C	never contacts his friends during his holidays
☐	D	likes to go on holiday abroad

Part (a)

(i) In the future, the man...

☐	A	will post a message about his holiday online
☐	B	will never book his holidays online
☐	C	will not post holiday photos online
⊠	D	will never reveal online that he is going on holiday	✓

91

(ii) The man lost...

⊠	A	all his possessions	✓
☐	B	details of his log-in
☐	C	his money when his holiday was cancelled
☐	D	everything he had saved online

Part (b)

(i) The woman was silly...

☐	A	to discuss animal testing online
⊠	B	to criticise her boss online	✓
☐	C	to advertise a watch online
☐	D	to post photos online

(ii) She...

☐	A	sent inappropriate emails
☐	B	advertised tickets for shows
⊠	C	lost her job	✓
☐	D	helped someone find a new job

Part (c)

(i) The boy...

☐	A	makes friends easily
☐	B	rarely uses the internet
☐	C	comes from a big family
⊠	D	has no siblings	✓

(ii) The boy...

☐	A	has lots of friends
⊠	B	hopes to make friends online	✓
☐	C	is going to subscribe to a new social network site
☐	D	wants to learn how to best use the internet

(Total for Question 8 = 6 marks)

92

Weather problems

9   You are listening to a report about weather problems in Mauritius on French radio.

Answer the following questions **in English**.

Part (a)

(i) What is the problem in Mauritius?
floods ✓   **(1 mark)**

(ii) For how long has the weather been an issue?
almost a month ✓   **(1 mark)**

(iii) Which towns and villages have been worst affected?
coastal (towns and villages) ✓   **(1 mark)**

(iv) What has happened to some inhabitants?
one of: lost homes / homes destroyed ✓   **(1 mark)**

(v) What new risk is there for some inhabitants?
(risk of dying of a) serious illness ✓   **(1 mark)**

(vi) What problem is being faced by aid organisations?
no access to airport ✓   **(1 mark)**

Part (b)

(i) How many French holiday-makers are on the island?
thousands ✓   **(1 mark)**

(ii) What will the French government try to do?
evacuate them ✓   **(1 mark)**

(iii) What has it already done? Give **two** details.
given financial help ✓ and sent food ✓

(2 marks)

(Total for Question 9 = 10 marks)

93

Être solidaire

10   Your hear Sophie and Vincent talking about world problems.
Put a cross ⊠ in each one of the **two** correct boxes for each question.

(i) What does Sophie say?

Example	Sophie says that we must respect the environment	⊠	
A	She is going to adopt a tiger	☐	
B	She only buys environmentally friendly products	⊠	✓
C	She has helped people with shopping	☐	
D	She is worried about world hunger	⊠	✓
E	She is going to take part in a demonstration	☐	

(2 marks)

(ii) What does Vincent say?

A	He has organised a fundraising activity	⊠	✓
B	He hopes to be able to give second-hand clothes to the homeless	☐	
C	A sale will take place in a few weeks' time	☐	
D	Vincent is proud of the people who have helped him	⊠	✓
E	He knows that he can do little to help the poor	☐	

(2 marks)

(Total for Question 10 = 4 marks)
TOTAL FOR PAPER = 50 MARKS

94

Set B Speaking Higher practice paper

Time: 22–24 minutes (total), which includes 12 minutes' preparation time

Role play
Topic: Travel and tourist transactions

Instructions to candidates

You are talking to an employee at a French tourist office. The teacher will play the role of the employee and will speak first.

You should address the employee as *vous*.

You will talk to the teacher using the five prompts below.

• where you see this – **?** – you must ask a question
• where you see this – **!** – you will have to respond to something you have not prepared

Task

Vous parlez avec un(e) employé(e) dans un office du tourisme en France.
1. Région – opinion
2. !
3. Durée des vacances
4. ? Les transports en commun
5. ? Sports dans la région

Prepare your answer in this space, using the prompts above. Then play the audio file of the teacher's part and speak your answer in the pauses. You can find a full sample answer of another student's response in the answer section.

Sample answers and teacher script

T: Bonjour. Que pensez-vous de notre ville?
P: Je trouve la ville très belle.
T: Ah oui. Qu'est-ce que vous avez fait hier?
P: J'ai visité le château.
T: Vous passez combien de temps ici en vacances?
P: Je passe une semaine ici.
T: Ah bon.
P: Comment sont les transports en commun en ville?
T: Il y a beaucoup de bus et les trains aussi sont fréquents.
P: Qu'est-ce qu'on peut faire comme sports?
T: Il y a un stade de foot, un centre sportif et une piscine.

95

Picture-based task
Topic: Cultural life

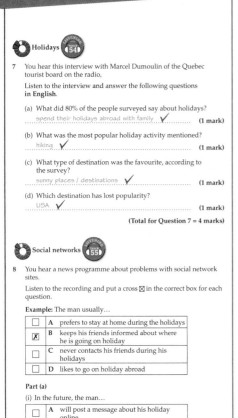

Regarde la photo et prépare des réponses sur les points suivants:

• la description de la photo
• ton opinion sur l'importance des fêtes nationales
• un mariage récent
• si tu voudrais te marier un jour
• !

Prepare your answer in this space, using the prompts above. Then play the audio file of the teacher's part and speak your answer in the pauses. You can find a full sample answer of another student's response in the answer section.

Sample answers and teacher script

• Décris-moi la photo.
Sur la photo il y a un mariage. Je vois le mari qui porte un costume et sa femme qui est habillée en blanc. Elle a des fleurs à la main et tout le monde est chic.

• Je pense que les fêtes nationales sont importantes. Quelle est ton opinion?
À mon avis, il n'est pas important d'avoir une fête nationale. Par contre, je crois qu'il est important d'avoir l'impression de faire partie de la société, car l'idée d'appartenir est essentielle de nos jours.

• Est-ce que tu es allé(e) à un mariage récemment?
Il y a deux mois je suis allé au mariage de ma cousine. Elle s'est mariée au bord de la mer, dans un château, et je me suis très bien amusé.

• Tu voudrais te marier à l'avenir?
Je me marierai un jour si je rencontre le partenaire de mes rêves et j'aimerais aussi avoir deux enfants. Je crois que le mariage est important pour montrer son amour.

• Comment est-ce que tu fêtes ton anniversaire normalement?
D'habitude, mes parents organisent une fête pour moi chez nous et je reçois des cartes et des cadeaux de ma famille et de mes copains. C'est génial.

96

130

Conversation

1 Qu'est-ce que tes parents font dans la vie?
2 Quel est ton emploi idéal? Pourquoi?
3 Quel travail est-ce que tu voulais faire quand tu étais plus jeune?
4 Quels sont tes plus grands accomplissements au collège?
5 Que penses-tu des échanges scolaires?
6 Tu fais partie d'un club au collège?

Prepare your answer in this space, using the prompts above. Then play the audio file of the teacher's part and speak your answer in the pauses. You can find a full sample answer of another student's response in the answer section.

Sample answers

1 Mon père est mécanicien et il aime bien son emploi car c'est bien payé. Par contre, ma mère, qui est secrétaire, trouve son travail assez barbant et elle voudrait être institutrice.
2 Mon emploi idéal serait médecin car je pourrais ainsi aider les malades. Je sais qu'il faut faire une formation longue et qu'on doit être très habile, mais j'aimerais bien essayer de suivre mon rêve.
3 Quand j'étais plus jeune, je voulais devenir astronaute parce que c'est un métier passionnant, ou peut-être joueur de foot professionnel, mais malheureusement je ne joue pas bien.
4 J'ai toujours fait de mon mieux à l'école, alors je suis fier de mes efforts. J'ai eu de bonnes notes dans plusieurs matières et j'ai aussi joué au foot pour l'équipe du collège.
5 Je n'ai jamais participé à un échange scolaire mais je voudrais en faire un jour, car je pense que je pourrais élargir mes horizons en découvrant la culture et le mode de vie d'un pays différent. Je pourrais aussi améliorer mes compétences linguistiques.
6 Je vais à un club d'athlétisme deux fois par semaine en été et je suis aussi membre du club de danse. Je pense qu'il est important de participer à des activités parascolaires.

97

Set B Reading Higher practice paper
Time: 1 hour

Total marks: 50

Answer ALL questions. Write your answers in the spaces provided. Some questions must be answered with a cross in a box ☒. If you change your mind about an answer, put a line through the box ☒ and then mark your new answer with a cross ☒.

SECTION A
Questions and answers in **English**

Using the internet

1 Read the article below.

> Nous avons demandé aux ados: << Pourquoi est-ce que vous utilisez Internet? >> Les réponses qu'on a reçues étaient intéressantes.
> • 95% des jeunes utilisent Internet tous les jours.
> • La majorité, c'est-à-dire cinquante-neuf pour cent, utilise Internet afin de faire des jeux. Certains y sont accros.
> • 50% regardent des clips vidéo, surtout les clips comiques, en ligne.
> • 35% tchattent sur des forums.
> • 30% téléchargent des chansons.
> • 25% font des recherches scolaires en ligne, mais on dit qu'ils acceptent trop facilement ce qu'on y met comme étant la vérité.
> • Moins de 5% disent qu'ils utilisent Internet pour se faire de nouveaux amis.

Answer the following questions in English. You do not need to write in full sentences.

(a) What percentage of young people interviewed play games online?
59% ✓
(1 mark)

(b) What do 30% of young people do, according to the survey?
download songs ✓
(1 mark)

(c) Which is the least popular reason in the survey for using the internet?
to make new friends ✓
(1 mark)

(Total for Question 1 = 3 marks)

98

A nightmare holiday

2 Read Millie's blog.

> Le jour du départ, l'aéroport de Montréal était entouré d'un brouillard épais et notre vol a été retardé, ce qui m'a vraiment énervée.
>
> J'ai trouvé le vol difficile car j'ai le mal de l'air, alors je n'ai rien mangé et le vol était tellement long!
>
> Enfin arrivés à Londres, on a eu du mal à trouver une voiture à louer car il y avait une grève. Mon père était de mauvaise humeur pendant le trajet en taxi de l'aéroport.
>
> Pour comble de malchance, nos chambres d'hôtel étaient sales, même si les repas au restaurant étaient délicieux et pas trop épicés.
>
> Je vais retourner à Londres le mois prochain avec mon équipe de tennis. J'espère que tout ira mieux!

Answer the following questions in English. You do not need to write in full sentences.

(a) Why was Millie's flight delayed?
fog ✓
(1 mark)

(b) What did she **not** do during the flight?
eat ✓
(1 mark)

(c) Why was her dad unable to hire a car?
there was a strike ✓
(1 mark)

(d) What did the family not like at the hotel?
the dirty rooms ✓
(1 mark)

(Total for Question 2 = 4 marks)

99

Being green

3 Read the magazine article.

> **Il est vraiment facile d'être plus écolo!**
> De nos jours, tout le monde parle de choses qui ne sont pas du tout concrètes comme le changement climatique, le réchauffement de la Terre ou l'empreinte carbone. La vérité, c'est que les gestes de toute la population menacent notre monde, mais il ne faut pas s'inquiéter car il existe toute une liste de choses qu'on peut faire afin de protéger la planète.
> Premièrement, un geste qui aide l'environnement mais aussi économise de l'argent, c'est réduire la consommation d'énergie. Éteignez la lumière en quittant une pièce et baissez le chauffage. Pour économiser de l'eau, essayez de toujours arroser les fleurs et les plantes du jardin avec l'eau de rinçage des légumes!
> Un autre problème grave c'est les déchets. Au supermarché, n'achetez pas les produits trop emballés et respectez la nature, par exemple ne jetez jamais des papiers par terre.
> De plus, choisissez plutôt les transports en commun au lieu de prendre la voiture et surtout, sensibilisez les jeunes en leur montrant le bon exemple, car il faut qu'à l'avenir ils fassent aussi un effort pour sauver notre planète!

Answer the questions in English. You do not need to write in full sentences.

(a) What benefit does the author say you could gain from saving energy?
save money ✓
(1 mark)

(b) What tip is given for saving water?
water plants with the water used to rinse vegetables ✓
(1 mark)

(c) What should you not buy at the supermarket, according to the article?
products with too much packaging ✓
(1 mark)

(d) What example is mentioned in relation to respecting nature?
don't drop litter on the floor ✓
(1 mark)

(e) What is the main advice given at the end of the article?
show young people a good example ✓
(Total for Question 3 = 5 marks)

100

Future plans

4 Read this blog by Suzanne on a Belgian website.

> Je vais bientôt finir mes études au lycée.
>
> Je vais prendre une année sabbatique. J'ai enfin pris la décision après y avoir longtemps pensé. Ce sera une expérience à la fois divertissante et enrichissante qui me donnera confiance, et aussi je deviendrai plus autonome, des aspects qui sont indispensable pour tous les êtres humains, à mon avis.
>
> Ayant fini mon année à l'étranger, peut-être en Afrique, je serai sans doute prête à recommencer mes études. J'ai des inquiétudes, c'est vrai. Par exemple, serai-je un peu isolée ou même aurai-je peur? Qui sait? Pourtant, je sais que je vais passer une année stimulante avant de travailler dur à la fac afin d'obtenir ma licence.

Put a cross ☒ in the correct box.

Example: Suzanne's time at school…

☐	A	has just ended
☒	B	will soon end
☐	C	was very pleasant
☐	D	seemed to last forever

(i) Suzanne's decision to take a gap year was…

☐	A	easy to make	
☒	B	a difficult one	✓
☐	C	influenced by her friends	
☐	D	influenced by her parents	

(ii) She thinks that doing a gap year will help her…

☒	A	be more independent	✓
☐	B	be more intelligent	
☐	C	earn more money	
☐	D	make new friends	

(iii) She feels that after her gap year she will…

☐	A	find university difficult	
☐	B	be unprepared for studying again	
☒	C	be ready to study again	✓
☐	D	have earned a lot of money	

101

(iv) She worries about…

☒	A	being lonely	✓
☐	B	making mistakes	
☐	C	getting lost	
☐	D	not understanding the languages spoken abroad	

(v) In the future she intends…

☐	A	to learn how to drive	
☐	B	to be a teacher	
☐	C	to find a well-paid job	
☒	D	to get a degree	✓

(Total for Question 4 = 5 marks)

102

131

Films

5 Read these views about films.

> On a cherché des opinions sur les films. Voilà quelques réponses!
> **Alice:** Je préfère regarder les films chez moi car c'est plus pratique. Chez soi, on évite les coups de pied dans le dos, les gens qui commentent tout haut, et les mangeurs de pop-corn bruyants. On peut y être plus à l'aise et faire ce qu'on veut. Je me passionne pour les films d'arts martiaux car j'y ai déjà trouvé quelque chose de profondément noble. Par contre, je ne supporte pas les films d'épouvante car selon moi ils sont une véritable perte de temps!
> **Bernard:** J'aime mieux sortir au ciné parce que le grand écran me plaît beaucoup et que j'aime bien rester silencieux en regardant un film. Dimanche, je vais aller au ciné revoir *Le dîner de cons*, même si c'est un film qui n'est pas vraiment destiné au grand écran, vu qu'il n'y a pas d'effets spéciaux et peu d'action.
> **Karine:** Selon moi les films romantiques sont abominables. Ce qui me plaît, c'est regarder un film où on peut s'identifier au héros ou à un espion. Hier on a vu *Chasse à l'homme* et c'était palpitant. Mes copains l'ont trouvé vraiment génial.
> **Lionel:** À mon avis, un film devrait divertir plutôt qu'informer ou enseigner. Je veux tout simplement choisir un film qui me permette de m'échapper du quotidien. Alors pas pour moi les documentaires ou les films qui cherchent à sensibiliser le public!
> Ce qui est certain, c'est que les films restent aussi populaires qu'auparavant chez les jeunes. Selon vos réponses, le plus important, c'est de se marrer avec des potes, le titre du film n'est pas toujours important.

Who says what about films?
Enter either **Alice**, **Bernard**, **Karine** or **Lionel** in the gaps below.

Example: ....Alice.... likes films which have noble intentions.

(a) ..Lionel.. ✓ wants to forget everyday life when watching a film. **(1 mark)**

(b) ..Alice.. ✓ hates horror films. **(1 mark)**

(c) ..Karine.. ✓ has recently seen an exciting film. **(1 mark)**

(d) ..Bernard.. ✓ is planning to see a film which he / she has already seen before. **(1 mark)**

Answer the following questions **in English**.

(e) According to the article's last paragraph, what has happened to the popularity of films amongst young people?
....stayed the same.... ✓ **(1 mark)**

(f) What is the most important consideration when watching a film, according to the responses of young people?
....having fun with mates / friends.... ✓ **(1 mark)**

(Total for Question 5 = 6 marks)

103

Le père Goriot by Honoré de Balzac

6 Read the extract from the text.
The author is describing a young woman, Victorine.

> Victorine est entrée dans le vestibule. Elle était très mince aux cheveux blonds. Ses yeux gris mélangés de noir étaient à la fois tristes et doux. Ses vêtements peu coûteux trahissaient des formes jeunes. Heureuse, elle aurait été ravissante et elle aurait pu lutter avec les plus belles jeunes filles. Il lui manquait ce qui crée la vraie beauté – elle n'était ni timide ni confiante. Son père croyait avoir des raisons pour ne pas la reconnaître, refusait de la garder près de lui, ne lui accordait que six cents francs par an, et avait dénaturé sa fortune, car il voulait la donner en entier à son fils. Parente éloignée de la mère de Victorine, qui jadis* était venue mourir de désespoir chez elle, Madame Couture, la propriétaire de pensionnat où elle vivait, prenait soin de l'orpheline comme de son enfant.
>
> *****jadis** = formerly*
>
> (Adapted and abridged from *Le père Goriot* by Honoré de Balzac)

(i) What do we learn from the text?
Put a cross ⊠ next to each one of the **three** correct boxes.

Example	Victorine entered the hall.	⊠
A	Victorine's eyes expressed conflicting emotions.	⊠ ✓
B	She is described as being shy.	☐
C	Her clothes were expensive.	☐
D	She seemed happy.	☐
E	She lacked something which prevented her being considered really beautiful.	⊠ ✓
F	She had a close relationship with her father.	☐
G	Her father wanted to give his son all his money.	⊠ ✓

(3 marks)

Answer the following questions **in English**.

(ii) What had happened to Victorine's mother?
....she had died (of despair).... ✓ **(1 mark)**

(iii) What role had Madame Couture taken in Victorine's life?
....a replacement mother for Victorine.... ✓ **(1 mark)**

(Total for Question 6 = 5 marks)

104

Être en forme en janvier

7 Lis le blog de Polly.

> Il vaudrait mieux ne pas boire d'alcool car c'est une drogue et il est très facile d'y devenir accro. Après avoir célébré Noël, on devrait se désintoxiquer. Il faudrait aussi qu'on retourne à la salle de sport afin de retrouver la forme, mais faites attention à ne pas faire trop d'exercice au début.
>
> Pourquoi ne pas suivre un régime? Consommez moins de sucreries et plus de nourriture bio, comme les légumes de saison. Comme ça on perdra du poids et on se sentira mieux.
>
> Ma sœur cadette, Daisy, est toujours vraiment mince, mais elle est accro au chocolat et elle en mange beaucoup tous les jours. Malgré ça elle ne prend jamais de poids. Quant à moi, si je ne fais pas attention à ce que je mange, je grossis facilement. Ce n'est pas juste car je mange du chocolat uniquement le week-end.

Mets une croix ⊠ dans la case correcte.

Exemple: Selon Polly, l'alcool…

☐	A	est bon pour la santé
☐	B	est facile à acheter
⊠	C	est comme une drogue
☐	D	ne présente pas de problèmes

(i) Polly dit qu'en janvier il vaut mieux…

☐	A	éviter les drogues
⊠	B	éviter le vin et la bière	✓
☐	C	éviter le tabac
☐	D	sortir trop le week-end

(ii) Elle dit que pour commencer, il faut…

☐	A	faire beaucoup d'exercice physique
☐	B	faire de la musculation tous les jours
⊠	C	commencer à faire un peu d'exercice	✓
☐	D	renoncer au sport

105

(iii) Selon elle, on doit…

☐	A	prendre du poids
☐	B	manger plus de sucre
⊠	C	consommer plus de légumes	✓
☐	D	éviter les légumes

(iv) Daisy…

☐	A	ne mange jamais de chocolat
☐	B	prend beaucoup de poids
☐	C	est assez grosse
⊠	D	mange du chocolat chaque jour	✓

(v) Polly…

⊠	A	pense que Daisy a de la chance	✓
☐	B	ne mange jamais de chocolat
☐	C	ne fait jamais attention à ce qu'elle mange
☐	D	est fille unique

(Total for Question 7 = 5 marks)

106

Les gîtes

8 Lis ces commentaires sur un site Internet.

La Corse:	Nous avons passé un séjour délicieux en Corse grâce au gîte exceptionnel qui était entouré d'arbres fruitiers de toutes sortes. Nous nous sentions comme chez nous et nous avons pu profiter du calme. Malheureusement le garage était fermé à clef.
La Bretagne:	Notre gîte n'avait pas assez d'équipements et nous étions déçus par l'absence de four à micro-ondes. Heureusement qu'on avait trouvé une piscine chauffée dans la région.
La Normandie:	Le gîte est mal insonorisé, donc il y avait trop de bruit venant de la route juste derrière le gîte. On est obligé de tout fermer si on veut bien dormir. La salle de bains est vraiment trop petite (minuscule lavabo, pas de tablette pour poser des produits de toilette).
La Provence:	Accueil chaleureux, rien à améliorer, tout est parfait. Nous y reviendrons et conseillerons cette étape autour de nous. Nous aimerions toujours trouver autant de gentillesse dans les gîtes. Encore merci!

C'est quel gîte? Choisis entre: **Corse**, **Bretagne**, **Normandie** et **Provence**.

Chacun des mots peut être utilisé plusieurs fois.

Exemple: L'accueil était super en ....Provence....

(a) La cuisine était mal équipée en ....Bretagne.... ✓ **(1 mark)**

(b) Il y avait de la circulation tout près en ....Normandie.... ✓ **(1 mark)**

(c) Il y avait plein d'arbres en ....Corse.... ✓ **(1 mark)**

(d) On va revenir au gîte en ....Provence.... ✓ **(1 mark)**

(e) On ne pouvait pas se laver facilement en ....Normandie.... ✓ **(1 mark)**

(Total for Question 8 = 5 marks)

107

Le stress à l'école

9 Lis cet article d'un magazine belge.

> **Le contrôle du stress**
> Il faut d'abord savoir que nous vivons tous un stress généré par nos conditions de vie. Il existe donc en nous, au départ, un certain niveau de stress qui contribue à améliorer notre rendement. Au-delà de ce niveau, la qualité de notre performance commence à baisser et le stress de l'examen ne fait que s'ajouter au stress déjà existant.
> En d'autres termes, selon ce qui vous arrive dans la vie, vous vous présentez à un examen avec un niveau de stress initial déjà plus ou moins élevé. Plus celui-ci est élevé, plus il sera facile de dépasser le niveau critique de stress. Si on ne fait pas d'effort pour diminuer le stress, on risque de ressentir une vraie panique!
> Il n'y a pas de mauvaises méthodes pour se détendre. Avant un examen, on devrait avoir assez de sommeil la veille et on pourrait faire de l'exercice physique ou même passer quelques bons moments en famille.
> Il peut être efficace de prendre quelques minutes pendant un examen pour vous rappeler un moment agréable que vous avez vécu, un moment de détente où vous vous sentiez particulièrement bien. Commencez par retrouver des images de ce souvenir au moment précis où vous vous sentiez bien; en d'autres termes, revoyez l'endroit où vous étiez. Puis, pensez aux bruits, aux sons associés à ce souvenir; enfin, retrouvez les autres sensations (détente, bien-être) que vous viviez à ce moment-là.

Réponds aux questions **en français**. Il n'est pas nécessaire d'écrire des phrases complètes.

(a) Selon l'article, qu'est-ce qui cause le stress?
....les conditions de vie.... ✓ **(1 mark)**

(b) Que faut-il faire la veille d'un examen?
....avoir assez de sommeil.... ✓ **(1 mark)**

(c) Que pourrait-on aussi faire avant un examen pour se détendre? Donne **un** détail.
....one of: faire de l'exercice / passer du temps en famille.... ✓ **(1 mark)**

(d) Qu'est-ce qu'on propose de faire pendant un examen?
....se rappeler un moment agréable du passé.... ✓ **(1 mark)**

(e) Pourquoi est-ce qu'on mentionne le bruit?
....il faut penser aux sons associés à un bon souvenir.... ✓ **(1 mark)**

(Total for Question 9 = 5 marks)

108

SECTION C

🔊 Translation

10 Translate this passage **into English**.

> Mes copains vont souvent à la patinoire dans la ville voisine. Il est embêtant de ne pas avoir une un peu plus près de chez nous. On vient de bâtir un nouveau centre commercial au centre. Pourtant, à mon avis, il vaudrait mieux qu'on construise un centre sportif car il n'y a rien à faire ici si on est jeune.

My friends often go to the ice rink ✓ in the neighbouring town ✓ . It's annoying not to have one a bit closer to our house ✓ . They have just built a new shopping centre in town ✓ . However, in my opinion it would be better ✓ for them to build a new sports centre ✓ because there is nothing to do here if you are young ✓ .

(Total for Question 10 = 7 marks)

TOTAL FOR PAPER = 50 MARKS

109

Set B Writing Higher practice paper
Time: 1 hour 20 minutes

Total marks: 60
Choose either Question 1(a) or Question 1(b)

Les passe-temps

1 (a) Dominique, ton ami(e) français(e), veut savoir comment tu passes ton temps libre.

Écris un e-mail à Dominique. Tu **dois** faire référence aux points suivants:

- tes émissions préférées à la télé
- ce que tu n'aimes pas faire et pourquoi
- une activité récente
- tes projets concernant un nouveau passe-temps.

Écris 80–90 mots environ **en français**.

J'aime regarder les émissions de télé-réalité car je les trouve amusantes, mais je préfère les documentaires sur les animaux, surtout en Afrique. Par contre, je déteste écouter de la musique parce que ce n'est pas intéressant, et je ne joue pas d'un instrument.

Samedi dernier, je suis allé(e) au ciné avec mon meilleur ami et nous avons regardé un bon film d'action qui m'a plu.

À l'avenir, j'aimerais bien essayer de faire de la planche à voile. J'aime les sports nautiques et je voudrais passer du temps au bord de la mer avec mes copains.

(Total for Question 1(a) = 20 marks)

110

La vie de tous les jours

(b) Un site Internet suisse pour les jeunes cherche ton opinion sur la vie de tous les jours.

Écris un article pour ce site Internet.

Tu **dois** faire référence aux points suivants:

- ta personnalité
- ce que tu aimes faire quand tu sors avec des amis
- un emploi que tu as eu
- tes projets d'avenir.

Écris 80–90 mots environ **en français**.

On dit que je suis très bavard(e) et aussi assez drôle et gentil(le), mais selon ma mère, je suis autoritaire. Quand je sors avec mes amis, j'aime surtout aller à la piscine où j'adore nager, et j'aime également faire les magasins en ville ou regarder un film.

Je travaillais dans un supermarché le samedi matin et c'était intéressant, mais maintenant j'ai trop de travail scolaire à faire, alors je n'ai pas de petit job.

À l'avenir, après avoir quitté l'école, je voyagerai beaucoup à l'étranger parce que j'aimerais découvrir des cultures différentes.

(Total for Question 1(b) = 20 marks)

111

Choose either Question 2(a) or Question 2(b)

Ma région

2 (a) Vous participez à une compétition organisée par le maire d'une ville en France.

Écrivez un article sur votre région pour intéresser le maire.

Vous **devez** faire référence aux points suivants:

- une description de votre ville/village
- votre opinion sur la région et pourquoi vous avez cette opinion
- une visite récente en ville
- l'importance du tourisme à l'avenir.

Justifiez vos idées et vos opinions.

Écrivez 130–150 mots environ **en français**.

J'habite dans une petite ville anglaise. Il y a plein de touristes, surtout en été, car ils viennent découvrir la campagne qui entoure la ville. Le centre-ville est assez animé et on peut y trouver des magasins, un nouveau centre sportif et un ciné.

J'aime bien ma région car elle est calme et pittoresque, mais il n'y a pas grand-chose pour les jeunes et il faut aller dans la plus grande ville voisine si on veut trouver une boîte de nuit.

La semaine dernière, je suis allé au ciné en ville avec mes copains. Après avoir regardé le film, qui m'a beaucoup plu, on a décidé d'aller manger dans un grand restaurant qui se trouve à deux pas de chez moi. C'était une soirée géniale parce qu'on s'est bien amusés.

Selon moi, le tourisme sera très important à l'avenir car il apporte une activité économique importante en attirant plein de visiteurs dans la région.

(Total for Question 2(a) = 28 marks)

112

Les vacances

(b) Un magazine belge cherche des articles sur les jeunes et comment ils passent les vacances.

Écrivez un article sur les vacances pour intéresser les lecteurs.

Vous **devez** faire référence aux points suivants:

- votre destination de vacances préférée et pourquoi
- ce que vous aimez faire en vacances
- des vacances difficiles que vous avez passées
- l'importance des vacances à l'avenir.

Justifiez vos idées et vos opinions.

Écrivez 130–150 mots environ **en français**.

Quand je pars en vacances, je préfère aller au bord de la mer car je peux me détendre. J'aime bien me faire bronzer à la plage ou lire un roman policier, allongé(e) près d'une piscine chauffée. De temps en temps je fais du vélo ou je vais en ville faire des achats, mais je n'aime pas les vacances actives parce que les vacances me donnent l'occasion d'oublier mes ennuis.

L'année dernière, on a fait du camping au pays de Galles et c'était désastreux. Il a plu tout le temps et on a dû rester sous la tente où je me suis vite ennuyé(e). Un jour, on a essayé de faire une excursion à la montagne mais la voiture est tombée en panne et mon père s'est fâché. Je ne voudrais plus jamais faire de camping!

À mon avis, il sera très important de passer des vacances à l'étranger à l'avenir, car il faut essayer de mieux comprendre les traditions et les cultures des autres.

(Total for Question 2(b) = 28 marks)

113

Translation

3 Traduis le passage suivant **en français**:

> I usually spend my free time at the seaside with my brother. Next weekend I'll go windsurfing but he will sunbathe on the beach. Last week I went to a classical music concert with my best friend. Her father took us there by car and we had a good time together.

D'habitude je passe mon temps libre au bord de la mer avec mon frère. Le week-end prochain, je ferai de la planche à voile mais il se fera bronzer sur la plage. La semaine dernière, je suis allé(e) à un concert de musique classique avec ma meilleure amie. Son père nous y a emmené(e)s en voiture et nous nous sommes bien amusé(e)s ensemble.

(Total for Question 3 = 12 marks)

TOTAL FOR PAPER = 60 MARKS

114

Published by Pearson Education Limited, 80 Strand, London, WC2R 0RL.

www.pearsonschoolsandfecolleges.co.uk

Copies of official specifications for all Pearson qualifications may be found on the website: qualifications.pearson.com

Text and illustrations © Pearson Education Ltd 2018
Typeset and illustrated by York Publishing Solutions Pvt. Ltd., India
Editorial and project management services by Haremi Ltd
Cover illustration by Miriam Sturdee

The right of Stuart Glover to be identified as author of this work has been asserted by him in accordance with the Copyright, Designs and Patents Act 1988.

First published 2018

21 20 19 18
10 9 8 7 6 5 4 3 2 1

British Library Cataloguing in Publication Data
A catalogue record for this book is available from the British Library

ISBN 978 1 292 23631 5

Acknowledgements
The author and publisher would like to thank the following individuals and organisations for their kind permission to reproduce copyright material.

Page 041, 121: « Les Daft Punk sont-ils fiers d'être français? » par Eléonore Prieur, publié sur lefigaro.fr le 13/02/2014 Copyright obligatoire © Eléonore Prieur / lefigaro.fr / 13/02/2014.
Page 050, 123: Reproduced with the permission of FranceAntilles.fr.
Page 108, 132: © Cégep à distance (www.Cégep à distance.ca).

Pearson acknowledges use of the following extracts:
Page 016, 117: Goscinny, René, *Le Petit Nicolas* (London: Longman, 1967).

Photographs
(Key: b-bottom; c-centre; l-left; r-right; t-top)

123RF: Cathy Yeulet 80, 128; **Alamy Stock Photo:** Axel Schmies/Novarc Images 96, 130; **Getty Images:** Franckreporter 24, 118; **Shutterstock:** Dubassy 11, 116, Dragon Images 38, 121, Rawpixel.com 67, 126.

All other images © Pearson Education

Notes from the publisher
1. While the publishers have made every attempt to ensure that advice on the qualification and its assessment is accurate, the official specification and associated assessment guidance materials are the only authoritative source of information and should always be referred to for definitive guidance.
Pearson examiners have not contributed to any sections in this resource relevant to examination papers for which they have responsibility.
2. Pearson has robust editorial processes, including answer and fact checks, to ensure the accuracy of the content in this publication, and every effort is made to ensure this publication is free of errors. We are, however, only human, and occasionally errors do occur. Pearson is not liable for any misunderstandings that arise as a result of errors in this publication, but it is our priority to ensure that the content is accurate. If you spot an error, please do contact us at resourcescorrections@pearson.com so we can make sure it is corrected.